american JUNK

american
JUNK

Mary Randolph Carter

Photographs by the Author

Design by

Marcia Weinberg Mossack

VIKING STUDIO BOOKS

VIKING STUDIO BOOKS
Published by the Penguin Group
Penguin Books USA Inc., 375 Hudson Street,
New York, New York 10014, U.S.A.
Penguin Books Ltd, 27 Wrights Lane,
London W8 5TZ, England
Penguin Books Australia Ltd, Ringwood,
Victoria, Australia
Penguin Books Canada Ltd, 10 Alcorn Avenue,
Toronto, Ontario, Canada M4V 3B2
Penguin Books (N.Z.) Ltd, 182–190 Wairau Road,
Auckland 10, New Zealand

Penguin Books Ltd, Registered Offices:
Harmondsworth, Middlesex, England

First published in 1994 by Viking Penguin,
a division of Penguin Books USA Inc.

Excerpt from *The Volcano Lover* by Susan Sontag. Copyright © 1992
by Susan Sontag. Reprinted by permission of
Farrar, Straus & Giroux, Inc.

CIP data available
ISBN 0-670-84400-4

Printed in USA

For my mother and father,
who have always looked beyond appearances for true worth

contents

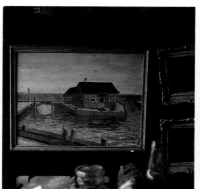

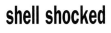

acknowledgments

Living with a junker, forager, or collector means living with someone else's clutter. My husband and two sons have lived with it all, shuddering every time we pass a roadside flea market, antiques shop, or tag sale. From an early age the boys covered my eyes when they spotted a junking zone of any sort. Little did they know that a true forager can smell a bargain a mile away. They never had a chance! Thank you, Howard, Carter, and Sam, for never saying "no." And thank you, Bo, for sitting patiently at my feet as I typed every word. You are a brave guard dog of the word according to junk!

For the Carter family (my parents, six sisters, and two brothers), collecting has always been a family sport. Our homes and get-aways, our barns, sheds, attics, basements, and storage spaces reflect our collective passion for hunting forgotten treasures. Father's old flooring, woodwork, locks, and doors are only rivaled by Mother's old books, paintings, furniture, chairs . . . you name it. Though each of us (thank goodness) has different kinds of manias, there have been family outings where we have all leapt on the same object—not a pretty sight! So thank you, Mother and Father, Cary, Nell, Jimmie, Emily, Liza, Bernard, Christian, and Cleiland, for sharing in all those expeditions that took us into the jumbled jungle of beautiful, beautiful junk. And a special thanks to Cleiland, who researched and discovered all manner of rescue tactics for everything from care-worn blankets to children's costumes.

Thank you also to Jean Berg, my mother-in-law, who has loved and cheered me on as though I were her own daughter.

Besides my real family, there is my second family, whom I work with Monday through Friday at Polo/Ralph Lauren. For the last several years, since I started work on American Junk, not a week has gone by when someone hasn't stopped by my office with the name of a junk palace or photos of a friend's collection. Best of all was my "junk" birthday party last year, when each member of my twenty-plus advertising team showed up with some of the worst stuff you've ever seen. So thanks, home team: Pat, Dedi, Marina, Ta, Polly, Mary A., Melissa, Mary D., Sonya, Natalie, Tracie, Tory, Beth, MJ, Cindy, Renee, Nancy, Liz, Ron, Kim, Cricket, Suzanne, and Deborah. And special thanks to Buffy Birritella, who has conspired with me in many ventures and on many adventures, and who has presented me with many a great find. And thank you to my faithful (she is the very definition of the term) friend and assistant, Ta Kimble, who has painstakingly helped me at every "junk-ture." And to Michael Morelli, one of the creative Wunderkinder at Polo, who, with Mark Campbell at Carlson and Partners (our advertising agency), has aided and abetted my junking habit with innumerable goodies and resources along the way—many thanks. Also at Carlson and Partners, thanks especially to Sandy, Jo, Karen, Kevin, Maia, and Chris.

The first time I met Ralph Lauren was at his office in his original brownstone headquarters at 40 West 55 Street. Every corner and wall were jammed and crammed with mementos from his children, friends, coworkers, and people he met on his travels. It was a wonderful, cozy hodgepodge that made me feel (as he did) comfortably at home. I asked him to write the foreword to my first book, American Family Style, and he accepted and reciprocated by inviting me to join his family at Polo. In six years, I have never wearied of watching his magic. Thank you, Ralph, for not only making the magic but sharing it, and for being a junk believer!

Thank you, Bruce Weber, for all the advice, leads, support, and friendship you have given me for so many years. Thank you, Barbara DeWitt (and all your gang), for everything, especially for introducing me to Alayne Patrick, who helped me comb the thrift stores of San Francisco, and to Terry Corrao, who chauffeured me to one junk site after another in Los Angeles. And thank you, Pam Barkentin Blackburn, for introducing me to Ron Meyer, whose secret garden and magic cottage will always be a treat to return to, and for introducing me to Laurie Warner and Eddie Garrick, whose multicolored bungalow is like a living piece of folk art. Thank you, Stephen Drucker, who always took my calls on his busiest closing days at The New York Times and who once ordered me to leave my office immediately and go downtown to visit the establishments of Judyth VanAmringe and Paula Rubenstein for total inspiration. You were right! And thank you to my dear friend Brigitte Lacombe, who not only let me invade her private lair but also introduced me to Lora Zarubin and Joan Juliet Buck.

Thank you, Susan Sontag, for The Volcano Lover and for permission to use part of it as the epigraph of this book, and for personally writing to me at home, which was such an unexpected thrill.

Thanks to Kimmel, the junking partner who goes beyond the call, and likewise to Sam and Gloria Landers, who have junked with me since the beginning of time, it seems, and have lately introduced me to new fields of junk in the mountains of North Carolina. And in Millerton, New York, to our good neighbors Elsie and Bob Albig, who have tipped me off to great local sales and events and have welcomed us almost every weekend with some sort of surprise from the garden—many thanks. Thank you, Joe Zullo, for all your feats—making a floor for my carriage-house bungalow, saving our barn, and never getting frustrated at change, change, change.

To all the friends of junk who contributed their collections, homes, and philosophies to the making of this book—thank you! In New York: Ellen O'Neill and her daughter, Bridget; Jerry Harmyck; Richard Giglio; Grace Coddington and Didier Malige; Sharone Einhorn; Kenny Kneitel; Doug Taylor; Kevin de Martine; Alice and Don Reid; Pauline Feli; Michael Fallon; Maralyn Marshall; Anne Keefe Chamberlin; Robert Miller and family; Fred Harris and Howard Frisch; and the Johnson family. In Los Angeles: Ron Meyer, Miriam Wosk, and Carol Hillman. In San Francisco: Judy Kaminsky; Big John; Deacon Willie Sharp; and Robert Miles Runyon and Claudette Runyon. In North Carolina: Jerry Pontes, Mr. Parker, and Charles Reber. In Florida: Tamara Hendershot. In Virginia: Cecil and Faye, Stuckey, Carol Ann, Zack and Ann, and Ellen and Morton Townsend.

And last but not least, thank you to two blood sisters. First, Marcia Weinberg Mossack, who lived and breathed and architected the look of American Junk in the same time it took her to get married to Robbie, find and redo an apartment, acquire a dog—Riley—and have a baby—Spencer. Which was easiest? Thank you, dear friend. And my editor, Barbara Williams, who always understands, knows what I'm trying to say and helps me say it better, props me up, keeps me believing, and makes me laugh—thank you, Barbara! And thank you to two blood brothers—Michael Fragnito, Publisher of Viking Studio Books, who believed in me the first time around with American Family Style but took a major leap of faith with Junk, and my agent, Steve Axelrod, who takes a major leap every time he hears from me.

And a final thanks to all those visionaries who had the good sense to rescue all those great American leftovers and put them out on their tag sale tables, flea market stands, thrift shop shelves, and rummage bins for all of us seekers of the cracked, tarnished, slightly worn, but beautifully authentic to discover and to treasure.

It is the entrance to a flea market. No charge. Admittance free. Sloppy crowds. Vulpine, larking. Why enter? What do you expect to see? I'm seeing. I'm checking on what's in the world. What's left. What's discarded. What's no longer cherished. What had to be sacrificed. What someone thought might interest someone else. But it's rubbish. If there, here, it's already been sifted through. But there may be something valuable, there. Not valuable, exactly. But something I would want. Want to rescue. Something that speaks to me. To my longings. Speaks to, speaks of. Ah . . .

—**Susan Sontag**
The Volcano Lover

what is junk?

Starting in my eighth summer, my family—my mother and father, three sisters, and a brother—and I, with my grandfather and three aunts, left the heat of our home in Richmond, Virginia, and moved for the season into an old barn, converted rather primitively into a house, which we called River Barn because of its proximity to the cool waters of the Rappahannock. Out back, between the house and the river, there was a small wooden storage house. Summer after summer, my sisters and brother (eventually there were nine of us—seven girls and two boys) and I would make a pretend home for ourselves among the lawnmowers, rakes, cans of oil, boxes of nails, chairs without seats—the tools and overages of a growing family. In the midst of this benign mess we would create tables out of boxes, stools out of barrels, beds out of old lawn furniture cushions and make believe it was all the finest. Tin cans would be our elegant bone china teacups. A paint-smattered dropcloth became an heirloom damask tablecloth. In a junk shop, like the one at left, I'm back among all that clutter searching for just the right thing that will stand in for something impossible to find or impossibly expensive. Two years ago it was the slightly chipped old red carnival vase on the floor at left, between the black wood stove and pink ice-cream maker. At $8, it made me totally confident I would find a place for it in our country house a few miles down the road (turn the page to see where it landed).

Left: The garage door (not the main entrance) to 22 Junk-A'Tique on Route 22 in Millerton, New York, is left open on hot summer days not only to welcome a breeze or two but to welcome stops by passing motorists, who can catch a clear view of the appetizing jumble due to the store's close proximity to the highway.

I must admit I never know exactly what I'm searching for until I spot it. Even with only a vague idea of how and where I might use it, I'm <u>absolutely positive</u> it's the right thing to have—<u>immediately</u>. In part, my instincts are guided by price. An $8 vase or anything in that range, though lacking provenance, is loaded with mystery. As my friend and fellow forager Ellen O'Neill once put it, "it is a purchase <u>without</u> angst." The decision to buy, then, is based on irrepressible desire with no thought to "Can I afford it." Value is self-determined. And, when I finally reach home and the new purchase looks terrible everywhere I put it (not the fate, fortunately, of my vase, seen in its new home at left), I'll have no regrets because I spent so little for it, enjoyed the hunt, and realize that by tomorrow or next week or in a year when I trip over it in my storage house it will be just the thing I need most at that moment.

Above: The object of my desire—a red glazed vase for $8—was found at 22 Junk-A'Tique on Route 22, one mile north of the traffic light in Millerton, New York. I didn't buy the pink ice-cream maker.

Left: After a good washing in warm soapy water, my vase found a home in the front parlor (my husband, Howard, calls it "the purposeless room"), on an old ship's card table surrounded with books. In autumn, it holds branches of leaves showing off their colors. In winter, it's long stems of pine and evergreens. In spring and summer, it's stalks of Queen Anne's lace and assorted wildflowers. The chipped mouth? Not to worry—it gives character!

In Collector's Luck in France, published in 1924, Alice Van Leer Carrick, in a series of letters to her friends back home—Louise, Isabel, Marie, and Theresa—relates marvelous tales of "shabby-shopping" in the French boutiques de curiosités: "tiny holes-in-the-wall where, if you have patience, you may find delightful trinkets for a song." The American equivalent, seventy years later, is hard to find. The hole-in-the-wall antique shops that collectors yearn for, if discovered, do not provide the bargains they once did. Collectors today must try their luck in alternative shopping environments, such as the thrift shops, rummage shops, trading posts, and anti-antique-priced establishments seen on these pages and throughout this book. Cluttered and jumbled with saucers, pots and pans, peeling shutters, bottles, beads, toys, mirrors, hats, trunks, hubcaps, and armies of hapless chairs, they are not unlike the Paris shops described by exhilarated Alice Van Leer Carrick—"an immense field of tangled possibilities."

Above: A station wagon can provide a surprising amount of room for found treasures. A pickup truck (aided by a few bungee cords) can go it one better. The only problem is: Where do the passengers go?

Above and top: Junk shops are stumbled upon in the most unlikely places. Consider, for example, the Rummage Shoppe on Route 22 in Millerton, New York. The only reminders of its days as a deluxe gas station in the fifties are the hubcaps displayed out front. The giant spider on the top was created by Stanley Johnson, the owner's oldest brother, out of old tailpipes. It's not for sale.

Left: The Union Jack Company in San Francisco entices urban rummagers with tables and baskets of sidewalk treasures. **Below:** Similar enticements outside Cecil's Antiques led me to rescue this frayed beauty for $20.

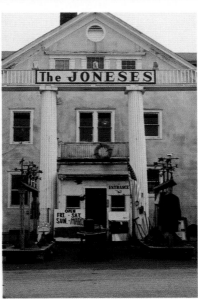

Above: The sign leaning in the window of the Rummage Shoppe in Millerton, New York, is the prayer of many a junk collector. **Above, center:** The sun shines down on a rare bargain—a $10 table—found on the third floor of Cecil's Antiques in Richmond, Virginia. **Above:** The Rummage Shoppe gets its name from that activity beloved by true foragers.

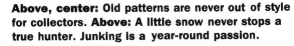

Above, center: Old patterns are never out of style for collectors. **Above:** A little snow never stops a true hunter. Junking is a year-round passion.

Above: Keeping up with Joneses is a challenge if what you're referring to is "The Joneses"—an indoor mall of collectibles shops that was housed in this huge stucco house graced with Tara-like columns in Great Barrington, Massachusetts.

flea markets offer collectors a breather—whether in beautiful countryside surrounded by hills and trees or in urban settings (a parking lot, most likely) surrounded by chain-link fencing and noisy traffic. A hard-core hunter opts for either with equal relish. Joan Juliet Buck, a writer whose talent with words may only be exceeded by her talent as a flea-market zealot, wrote in an article in HG magazine in March of 1990: "Going to flea markets is the only sport that interests me, a form of urban hunt that combines the illusion of freedom with the need for stealth. Flea markets also provide fresh air and a decent amount of exercise and demand a mental attitude that can otherwise be attained only in the higher stages of Zen; calm attention, a drifting tolerant curiosity and an openness to whatever crosses the mind's eye and the hand's touch."

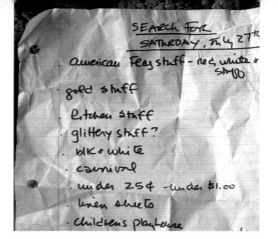

For the Junk Hunt: Essential Tools

- <u>A magnet</u>: For testing metals. A magnet won't stick to "pot" metals or brass.
- <u>A small magnifying glass</u>: To look for chips, cracks, dates, marks, names of artists, and manufacturing trademarks.
- <u>A Swiss army knife or good pocket knife</u>: The little scissors are very handy.
- <u>A pen and paper or notebook</u>: For keeping track of purchases and how much you spend. (Receipts sometimes get lost, or you can't read the handwriting.) I tape in dealers' cards and make notes on the shop or its wares. You never know when you might want the very things it specializes in.
- <u>A list</u>: Of what you're hunting for is incredibly helpful, particularly at a large flea market, where things can get a little overwhelming. That doesn't mean you can't stray from what's listed, but it can keep you focused.

Junking Survival Kit

- <u>Wash'n Dri towelettes</u>: Indispensable after handling a lot of grimy stuff. Though you may be lucky enough to find a toilet, normally it's hard to find a sink. (A small pack of tissues is also handy when the Portosan has run out of toilet paper.)
- <u>A cooler in the car filled with bottled water, juices, carrot sticks, fruit, and yogurt</u>: For a long day of junking, particularly if you're driving from shop to tag sale to flea market. You won't want to waste time stopping for food. Also, you don't have to add junk food to junk hunting. Eat a good breakfast in the morning.
- <u>Sunblock and some form of aspirin</u>: A good idea, depending upon the weather.
- <u>A Polaroid or small camera</u>: For keeping a record of what you bought or for recording things you didn't buy but loved. I don't suggest lugging a heavy one around with you all day. Kodak's disposable cameras are the perfect size and weight.

Money

There's lots of stuff out there for a dollar or two. Take along twenty singles and a few fives or tens. Some people don't like to make change, or don't have it, and sometimes cash can get you a better deal. Take a major credit card, your driver's license for identification, and a bunch of checks.

Junk Dressing

- Comfortable clothes are the rule.
- If you'll be outside, dress in layers. Don't wear a heavy coat you can't get rid of.
- Never carry a pocketbook. I fold my money, a credit card, and driver's license into the pockets of one of the many fishing vests I have collected for my favorite sport—junking. An alternative is a bag that you strap around your waist.
- Wear a hat to keep the sun off your face. I prefer a fishing hat with an elongated bill or a baseball hat.
- Sunglasses tend to get in the way. I'm always taking them off to scrutinize something. If you want them, I suggest attaching them to a cord that can hang around your neck.
- Some people suggest a lightweight fold-up poncho in case it rains. I usually take my chances.
- Flea-market fields can get very muddy, but boots (alas!) can get very hot and heavy (unless you can keep them in the trunk and retrieve them and your rain gear as needed). An old pair of sneakers or something you don't care about might make more sense.

Haggling

I always ask a dealer if she can do better, unless, of course, the item is really cheap or seems fairly priced. Before I bargain, I make a pile of things I'm interested in. A dealer is more apt to make a deal on a group of things than a single item.

Junking Solo or Ensemble

Most diehard junkers are loners. They want no distractions, no lagging behind, and no competition. I must admit to having these tendencies, but junking with my mother, sisters, and good friends is always a load of fun. The bad thing, of course, is when you fixate on the same things. (We have a "who grabs it first gets it" code.) There's also the well-meant "You <u>have</u> to buy it" incantation, which often leads one to leap before looking. But, on the other hand, it is often helpful to have someone else's honest opinion.

Restraint

When I go into a shop or large flea market I try to peruse the whole place at least once. I check out the things that make my heart beat faster, and then go back and start asking questions. There are times I have lost something I loved because I held back. Listen to your heart.

junk transcends all decorating styles. Though junk collectors are apt, sometimes, to be on the defensive, and say they never collected anything valuable, what they probably mean is valuable in <u>someone else's eyes</u>. The beauty of junk is truly in the eye of the beholder. This book encourages that kind of self-confidence and the style born out of it, which is very personal, very authentic, oftentimes thrifty, and seldom accomplished without a great deal of mirth. There are lessons on how to bargain, overcome chips and snags, how to camouflage, and how to hunt happily ever after for the worth of the worthless, the usefulness of the used, and splurge $5 on something totally outlandish that you really and truly love!

Right and above: One Sunday, a few hours before I discovered my little stone Infant of Prague amid the secondhand bric-a-brac of my favorite country thrift shop, I'd seen another one at the back of the little church I attend in Lakeville, Connecticut. When later I saw this one in The Rummage Shoppe in Millerton, I was startled not only at the coincidence, but also at the price— $1. He now lives happily ever after on the mantel in our country-house parlor.

western junk

To be a cowboy and live under the big sky with horse, hat, and holster is a dream particularly American. The stories of Zane Grey, the bronzes of Remington, the photographs of Ansel Adams, and, lest we forget, the movies of silver screen heroes like John Wayne, seen opposite, inspire many into collecting for their own make-believe frontier lands. Supporting that dream are antiques dealers like Pauline Feli, whose obsession for things of the West has filled up her shop, an old barn at an upstate New York flea market. It provided the props necessary to transform a venerable New England carriage-house stall (see pages 12–19) into a full-fledged bunkhouse getaway. On the West Coast, cowboy dreams are launched at "swap meets." Some, like the one held the second Sunday of each month at the Rose Bowl in Pasadena, are practically institutions. "But don't discount yard sales," puts in Laurie Warner, a Los Angeles artist and collector, who offers as proof the cowboy lamp, seen on page 20, that she drove by and spied, then kept going, thought again, and backed up for. It is just one of the many rewards of diligent sightings, including those made by her husband, Eddie, that have given new meaning to their "ranch" house from the fifties. Luck and a little aggression never hurt in the hunt for the unusual. Doug Taylor, a fellow forager who has set up shop in Guilford, New York, kicks himself daily for the ones he left behind. "If you can't, or think you can't, live without it, don't be cool and walk away—go for it!" His buckaroo suite (see pages 24–27), tucked in the attic of his bed-and-breakfast home—a Greek Revival mansion—is testimony to that kind of instinct.

Left: True grit intact, America's number-one hero of the West stands his ground amid the clutter of Pauline Feli's upstate New York shop— Stepping Stones.

Top and above: Behind the classic facade of our carriage house is a western fantasy room—once a horse stall—guarded by a splintery chair (seen again at right), found at a flea market for $20.

Above: A truckload of western junk booty —furniture, floor coverings, and cowboy bric-a-brac, rounded up at a local auction for less than $500—awaits its next life in my bunkhouse study.

Above and right: The tilting landscape, picked up for a mere $10, hangs more confidently above that splintery chair, softened by a pillow covered with a mighty elk case ($10 from a flea market).

It was a space-starved city slicker's fantasy come true—a pristine white two-story two-hundred-year-old carriage house (see opposite page, lower left) complete with cupola, 1,500 square feet, two horse stalls, and lofty ceilings—a bonus with the nearby house we had recently acquired for weekends away from New York City. And it was totally empty! My husband stared and thought, "Garage space." Our two sons, scrambling up to where the hay loft had been and spying an old basketball rim, declared it their own Madison Square Garden. I, giddy from the sheer luxury of uncluttered, unclaimed nothingness, conjured up a new home for all those countless treasures, collected for years at junk shops and flea markets. A second fantasy began on the earthen floor of one of the stalls, where horses had once stamped and rubbed their backs against old, warm wood. I dreamed of a little summer study that would feel like a bunkhouse in Montana, furnished with odd western stuff. The groundwork, a rough pine floor, was laid by a local craftsman in a day. The furnishings took a little longer.

Opposite page, clockwise from top left: A mock-majolica pitcher, picked up at a roadside tag sale for $4. Two hours of patient waiting at a local country auction and bidding more than I wanted ($125) won me this peeling painted-twig rocker. The fabric-covered sewing stool at its feet was scooped up in much less time, at a local Grange flea market for $3. "Banff" and "Alta," hand painted onto this rough leather book cover, conjure up what the missing contents must have been—photographic memories of two great mountain holidays. These seven volumes of works by Zane Grey were a bargain at $50. The little pair of boots hold a pencil and eraser each, a gift from a cowgirl friend. Framed in old brass frames, and matted with corrugated cardboard, magazine tearsheets make charming folk-art fakes for less than $1 apiece, as shown at left. The clay sombrero, a souvenir ashtray from Mexico, was spotted on a cluttered table at a roadside tag sale for 50 cents. I spied the sage-colored wreath on the outside of an old junk shop. I pulled in and asked the owner if he would sell it. Sold at $3! Lesson: never hesitate to ask! My horse-stall hideaway cost me less than $300 to furnish, and another $400 for the works of art, maps, books, and authentic and not-so-authentic stuff that dreams _and_ dream places are made of.

Above: Virginia Woolf wrote, "In order for a woman to write fiction she needs money and a room of her own." She failed to mention that you also need a desk. The one pictured above and to the far left was discovered in the dimly lit attic of a going-out-of-business junk shop about seven years ago, for $45. It was crudely made by a resourceful backwoods teacher, and its distinctive feature—a slant-top lectern lid—now boards a white metal stallion and, to its left, a wooden photo album, a souvenir from an amusement park. Both were bargained from a favorite dealer for $35 (not such a bargain) and $2 (a bargain), respectively. The red wooden postcard holder, decoupaged with bucking broncos, was picked up in a San Francisco shop, Pink Paraffin, for $5.

Top: A view of the study from the inside stall door. The large map of the United States on the back wall, from a 1940s schoolroom set of three, pulls down from a wooden rack that was usually mounted above a blackboard. The three were purchased for $185. The birdhouse at right, with two chewed-out entrances, cost me $300 at auction. Hovering above is an owl decoy left by the former owners. Tacked to the left of the map are two color vignettes of General Custer. The oil painting below, from a porch sale, reminded me of the Australian homestead in the film <u>My Brilliant Career</u>. The bamboo coffee table, part of a set from the 1930s, cost about $15. The pink-and-white ladderback chair with a plywood seat was $20. The metal milking stools, picked up at tag sales, were $5 and $10. The pair of Beacon blankets from the forties (seen opposite) were gifts.

Left: Against the backdrop of a Beacon blanket from the forties, the best of the West—Zane Grey and Edna Ferber.

Blanket Approval: How to Buy and Care for Old Beacons and Pendletons

In the late nineteenth century, Pendleton Mills was the only company that manufactured woolen blankets and shawls strictly for Native Americans. Beacon Manufacturing, established in the early 1920s, produced a lighter blanket, of wool and cotton. Those at left and above, Beacons from the 1940s, are a cotton-acrylic blend. "One of the signs of a synthetic blend, which dates it as a later blanket, is the way it pills," notes Paula Rubenstein, a collector and owner of Paula Rubenstein Antiques in New York City. Prices today are determined by age, condition, and the specific pattern of the blanket. Paula's sell for anywhere from $100 to $450. Dry cleaning is her favored method for sprucing up old blankets. Robert Kapoun, the author of <u>Language of the Robe</u> and owner of The Rainbow Man, a shop in Santa Fe, New Mexico, suggests caring for an old wool blanket as you would a favorite old sweater—"Woolite it in cold water, and let it air dry." Laurie Warner (see page 20) has successfully machine-washed new Pendletons in cold water "as many as fifty times" in order to soften their feel and colors.

Far left and above: With the exception of the "Marlboro man" hat, which was bought in a gallery in Los Angeles, the whole collection on this wall cost $44.50. The cuckoo clock, which doesn't work, came out of a box lot at an auction for $5. Below it is a pair of portraits, in frames of coconut bark decorated with woven palm. I paid $12 for the pair. The rearing horse to the left of the hat was cut out of a magazine and framed. I paid $1 for it, and $20 for Hiawatha and his bride, to the right of the hat and in the big picture above. The "Cowboy in Winter," another magazine cutout framed below the horse, cost $6. All three came from Stepping Stones. The landscape, in what looks like a tinfoil frame, came from a man who got it as part of a big lot at an auction. He was thrilled to get rid of it for $5.

Above: Another view of my horse-stall retreat reveals, through its open door, an old two-wheeler from the forties (a Victory I pedaled off and away with from a Copake, New York, auction for $75) and another stall across the way, now a storeroom for winter wood. Before the previous owners changed the space, there were five box stalls here. Each horse had its own little window.

Opposite, bottom right: Above the pink-and-white chair, seen in the view of the stall at top, is a little carved shelf and a quartet of wooden napkin rings that I picked up at one of the flea markets run by the Copake auctioneer Michael Fallon when he needs to purge his warehouse. I cut the two primitive sketches framed on the back of the shelf out of an old <u>Life</u> magazine. All five finds cost $3. The still life of peaches, a printed illustration glued on Masonite, was bought at a tag sale for $2.

Right: Until around 1968, a real horse stood in the spot where this old school desk stands, displaying a slightly wobbly cast-iron stallion and a copy of <u>The Twins in the West</u>, a tale of adventure published in 1920. I coralled the horse, a decorative piece popular in the fifties, for $12 from Pauline Fell's collection of western kitsch at Stepping Stones. The print of a landscape with a little house overlooking a babbling brook reminded me a little of my view just outside. It also came from Stepping Stones for $3. The yellowed enamel bowl rimmed in green and its matching covered container, circa 1930, were tag-sale pickups for $2.

In 1984, Laurie Warner, an artist and one-of-a-kind furniture designer with an insatiable appetite for color, texture, and pattern, often bringing home the odd thing she couldn't pass up, and, on top of that, a mother and grandmother who ''always collected stuff—the legitimate way to express one's personality, they taught me!''—met Eddie Garrick, a film director, producer, and traveler to ''National Geographic kinds of places.'' On these trips he began ''years ago'' to be attracted to the colors, textures, and patterns of tribal masks, paintings, and sculpture—''folk art from all over.'' Slowly but surely they fell in love. In 1991, they got married, and Laurie moved her collections into Eddie's bachelor digs, a funky California ranch house tucked into a hillside just off a twisty Laurel Canyon road in Los Angeles. ''From the outside, it's not a remarkable house,'' they admit, but in the works is a remarkable 18-color paint job to make the outside match the riot of color just beyond the threshold of their turquoise front door.

Far left: To one side of the front door stands a weathered, close-to-life-size painted plaster-mold cowboy lamp, which Laurie screeched on the brakes for at "the one and only garage sale" she's been to. (After finding this dude for $25, how could she have stopped?) Eddie found the lamp shade later at a folk-art/junk shop in Pasadena for another $25. Laurie describes it as "one of those little home-project kind of shades," made out of rocks set in resin. The iridescent paper bandana was tied around the cowboy's neck in memory of Laurie's grandmother. "She once tied it in her hair. You had to know my grandmother. She was a very dignified woman. It was such a wonderful moment—" and, in its new spot, such a warm memorial.

Above: Just within the cowboy sentry's ken is a table topped with Laurie's "snowies" collection. "Tales of Eddie's college collection of 300 snowies inspired me to collect my own." The earliest—from the thirties—was given to her by her mother. The others were picked up in airports all over. The sofa, from Eddie's bachelor days, is tucked with Pendleton blankets (see blanket tips on page 17). The pillow on the left is wrapped in a piece of Guatemalan fabric. The piece that makes this room, they both agree, is the little canoe floating in the window, a 1940s tourist souvenir from the Northwest Coast. The quartet of Native American figures (one holding a tiny umbrella) was swooped up from a favorite shop in Santa Monica for $5 apiece.

Top, far left: Another view of the living room, where Eddie's collection of tribal masks from the Solomon Islands, New Guinea, New Mexico, and the Pacific Northwest predominates. The small table to one side of the sofa is a Laurie Warner original. The floor lamp behind it was home made from a cactus skeleton. Eddie brought the banner on the wall back from Haiti.

Top left: Eddie's old sofas didn't know what hit them once Laurie moved in—a Pendleton blanket and a corner of eclectic pillows collected by Laurie from as far away as Vermont, where she found the castles painted on velvet for $20. The Native American appliquéd on velvet was $35. The little painting propped up at the far right was sold to Laurie by a homeless woman for $16.50.

Below left: A tabletop altar to glitz and shine, dominated by a memory jar from at least 1919, as attested to by the little Red Cross button in the center. The jar (actually empty) is encrusted with stray buttons, pebbles, a four-leaf clover, a locket—the stuff found floating loose in pockets and odd drawers. Laurie discovered this treasure at a folk-art gallery in Santa Monica. Resting on top is a Christmas ornament made by her grandmother. The cross, made by a prisoner from sheet metal, was found at the same gallery. The stained-glass glasses hold candles for New Year's. Partially hidden behind them is an acorn-pit bowl of sequined Styrofoam balls. The beaded flowers were another handmade-by-Grandmother gift.

Above right: An ingenious way to keep marbles from underfoot— glue them onto an old cane . . . Not! Well, Laurie and Eddie found the deed done, and irresistible at $200, at a gallery in Chicago.

Below right: "I have so many little things," says Laurie with a sigh, "that I find it easier—on Eddie, too!—to keep them all together in my studio." Her bookshelves have become populated with small worlds of people, animals, vehicles, and buildings made of wood, cardboard, and tin. Artfully arranged—"not intentionally," Laurie asserts—they form a tribute to the collector.

doug Taylor is a hoarder from way back. "My mother recently reminded me that when I was seven and we lived in Saint Louis, in one of the recently built suburbs, I couldn't wait for the first Thursday of the month, when everyone put their 'big trash' out on the sidewalk. Everyone was so into 'new' then that you could find really great stuff in very good condition. I remember bringing home a really terrific ukulele and an amazing book on the Saint Louis Zoo." When he worked as a graphic artist in Chicago, and eventually New York City, his obsession continued and became a constant inspiration. "I always loved the funny little drawings on old matchbook covers." Several years ago, Doug gave up city life and moved to a farm in upstate New York, where there was "more space for hoarding and a nice quiet place to work." Soon the idea dawned on him to open a bed-and-breakfast, which precipitated the purchase of a Greek Revival house, circa 1840, located smack dab in the middle of quaint Guilford, New York, prime B-and-B territory (and prime junk territory, too). Across the street from the B-and-B (named The Village Green), in an old church, Doug has made a business out of his obsession—Praiseworthy Antiques. The shop's card reads "Oh, please, Lord, let me find it here." "Having a sense of humor about all this stuff is really important," quips Doug. "Once you get too serious, it's no fun."

Left: When Doug Taylor's mother heard that the room he had chosen for his very own (out of the house's fourteen) was the chauffeur's attic room over the kitchen, she just laughed. "It's my hideaway from guests and the formality of the rest of the house," Doug retorts. The cozy three-room suite, with its original wainscoting, "is filled with the stuff that's most dear to me." The pair of bird's-eye maple beds were found in a local secondhand store for $60. Doug bought the Hudson Bay blankets from a dealer ("I never pay more than twenty dollars per"). The kilim rug only looks like a Navajo. The stag paintings on either side of the window are paint-by-number studies that cost $2 for the pair. The Emeralite green glass shades were about $25 when he found them years ago. "Now they go for as much as seven hundred. Forget it!"

Above: Among the one-of-a-kinds displayed between the beds is, at left, a Boy Scout's proud project—a painted snake mounted on plywood, probably the insignia for the scout's patrol, which was purchased for 50 cents. The box it rests on, found in a New York City flea market for about $40, supposedly belonged to an itinerant tattoo artist. The different-sized drawers accommodated assorted tools and designs. Inside the ink-stained drawers, Doug found stickers from tattoo suppliers. The Indian maiden pinup reminds Doug of one of his hugest mistakes. She was one of a collection of fifteen or twenty plywood beauties in different costumes and poses, found for $10 apiece at the Twenty-sixth Street flea market in New York City. "I can't believe I left them there!" The kneeling Indian burdened by a wooden Mountie, placed there in jest by Doug, originally rode a horse. The open box under the Indian was originally designed to hold the 78-RPM records of an aspiring western singer. On either side are carved figures of people in western garb. "It cost ten dollars at a flea market up here."

Right: The maple-leaf pinups over Doug's bed—"really weird"—were bought about five years ago for $5. The painted chalkware deer head above them cost $2 at Mike Toby's in South New Berlin, New York. "Mike always hangs the really odd stuff on the wall behind his desk. That's where I spotted it."

Left and above: Blocking the door to the bedroom is a birch lamp from the Adirondacks. "I bought it because I needed a tall one," reports Doug. "It didn't really seem very special until the birds came to perch. They were a collection I decorated my Christmas tree with each year." To the left of the lamp, atop a fruit-box chest of drawers, are more trees—a miniature forest from an Alice in Wonderland set. The little bone-and-pitch dinosaur in front, with an abalone fetish in its mouth, was found in the Southwest, the work of the eight-year-old son of a Native American craftsman. "I once left it too near a radiator and it melted." The smaller pair of cowboy boots on the floor was 75 cents. The larger pair was a mistake. "I bought them at full price from one of those Madison Avenue cowboy stores. They never fit. So, they've become a very expensive prop." (More on Doug and the jacket and creel on page 72.)

Above: Bottle Shop Antiques, located in a late-nineteenth-century carriage house in Washington Hollow, New York, is open for business daily come snow or come shine.

In upstate New York, east of the Taconic State Parkway at the Millbrook exit, around a rather sharp turn in what is known as Washington Hollow, you'll see to your right a wooden bottle-shaped sign announcing the driveway of Bottle Shop Antiques. The proprietor, Kevin de Martine, started selling bottles on the same spot more than twenty-five years ago, when he was fourteen. He and his cousin would dig up old bottles and jars back in the woods at abandoned building sites, wash them, and line them up on a table near the road—"sort of like a lemonade stand," Kevin suggests. (For a peek at what one of those dug-up treasures might have looked like, turn to page 33 and gaze upon my most prized bottle, described by Kevin as "sick.") Later, his hunt took him to auctions, where he expanded his collection to include crocks and tools and eventually an endless list of things that spill out from the double doors of the late-nineteenth-century carriage house (see above) that he opens daily from ten to five. The chorus line of bottles on the previous pages represents an inexpensive assortment ("Nothing particularly exceptional," insists Kevin) of easy-to-finds.

Left: At Stuckey's Antique Emporium in Richmond, Virginia, a tall glassy amazonian woman—a French figural liquor bottle that sold for $25—holds in her arms (one's patched together with tape) what appears to be a giant boa constrictor, as a wise old owl to her left, a carnival glass bottle ($22), and a plaster-of-paris painted bird ($18) look on.

Previous pages: Starting in the shadows at the far left is a group of figural bottles that held fruit syrup (a precursor to Kool-Aid) manufactured in the forties and fifties. (The term "figural" designates any bottle crafted in a recognizable shape—animate or inanimate.) From left to right are Abraham Lincoln, Carrie Nation, another Lincoln, a bear, George Washington, Mr. Pickwick, and a fox. Figural bottles like these often came with slotted caps that had a cardboard insert underneath, so that after the contents were used pennies could take their place. The second Lincoln bottle from the left, the bear, the fox, and the squat Nash's mustard jar from the 1930s (seen to the far right in front of the fish, a cod-liver oil bottle) are all similarly fitted. To the fish's right is a bust of George Washington—a reproduction of a Simon's Centennial Bitters bottle from the 1950s. The historical eagle flask, to the left of the fish, was sold with Lestoil in it in the fifties. A Heinz catsup bottle from the 1880s stands to its left. The only jar in the picture, seen at the far right, is a Horlick's malted-milk jar from 1910. Next to it is a dark brown demijohn that once held vinegar. All bottles and the jar are machine made and range from $5 to $20.

Bottle Tips for Beginners

Age: According to the Encyclopedia of Collectibles: Beads to Boxes, published by Time-Life Books, most bottles made between 1810 and 1910 were crafted by hand. These are the ones serious collectors are after. Early hand-blown bottles have a "pontil scar" on the bottom where the glassblower's rod left a sharp-edged chunk of glass. Bottles hand-blown between 1845 and 1870 exhibit a circular black, red, or white mark on their bottoms from fragments of the oxidized iron deposited by the heated pontil. Molded bottles can be dated by observing the length of the seam left by the mold. The higher the seam, the later the bottle. Kevin de Martine suggests that any bottle with lots of bubbles in the glass is "an old one."

Colors: Cobalt blue, red, green, amber, or any unusual shade contributes to the value of a bottle. There are several good guides to pricing and identifying bottles. I found Bottle Pricing Guide by Hugh Cleveland helpful because there were so many pictures. Copies can be ordered for $7.95 from Collector Books, P.O. Box 3009, Paducah, Kentucky 42001. Add $2 for postage and handling.

Condition: Try to avoid buying bottles that are chipped, cracked, or "sick"— that is, have come into contact with organic materials in the soil and environment that cause a foggy, cloudy, or discolored look. Some sick bottles, like the one seen opposite, top left, can be quite beautiful. Bottles with paper labels intact are more valuable than those without. Unusual embossing adds to a bottle's value—"the more outrageous the better," says Kevin.

Care: A really sick bottle can be soaked in ammonia water (four parts water to one part ammonia) or Cascade dishwasher detergent. Good bottle brushes are a must, but hard to find. If a brush won't fit, a handful of BBs can be slowly rolled inside the bottle and the bottle eventually rinsed out with distilled water. To dry the inside of a narrow-mouthed bottle, insert a tightly rolled piece of paper towel into the bottle, leaving one end exposed to the air. It should eventually soak up the moisture. White vinegar is said to remove alkaline deposits.

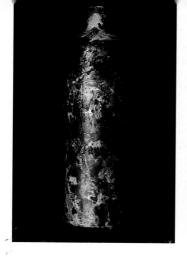

Far left: This beautiful "sick" bottle was bought at Bottle Shop Antiques for several dollars. The rainbow discolorations were caused by contact with organic materials in the soil, where it was most likely found.

Left: Old or new, all bottles look great with a little sunlight streaming through them. These, for sale at a roadside thrift shop in upstate New York, were offered for between 50 cents and $2.

Above: Though the Jim Beam family has been in the business of distilling whiskey since the eighteenth century, it wasn't until Christmas of 1953, when they started selling their Kentucky Straight Bourbon in special decanters, that they forever endeared themselves to bottle collectors. Since then, series after series of themed collections and commemorative specials created out of fine Regal china have inspired bottle-collecting zealots to fill their shelves with the kind of novel creations seen above at the Motherway Boutique on Fillmore Street in San Francisco. From the "state" series, an erupting volcano on the top shelf, far left, immortalizes Mount St. Helens in Washington State. The donkey and elephant on the lower shelf, from the 1956 "political" series, were designed to be used as ashtrays once emptied. The prices for the hundreds of Beam bottles listed in Hugh Cleveland's 1992 Bottle Pricing Guide range from as little as $4 to as much as $3,000 for a 1970 Spiro Agnew elephant.

Above: Figural bottles like the pair seen in our New York City apartment—a matador and a Spanish dancer—have delighted collectors since ancient times. This 12″ pair, which I collected at a flea market more than ten years ago for $5, once served Spanish brandy. His broken right arm definitely detracts from his value today, which, according to a 1992 bottles price list, would be $45 with a good arm.

Left: Mrs. Butterworth, out of syrup but in bloom with giant artificial sunflowers, was a gift from our neighbors in the country, Elsie and Bob Albig. According to my 1992 bottles price list, she could have cost as much as $8. The mountain still life above her cost a quarter at a local rummage shop. The miniature stein to her left, a souvenir of Niagara Falls, cost 50 cents at a secondhand shop. The photographer under the furry cap? Yours truly in junk —M. R. Carter!

Top right: My desk at home in New York City is an old country worktable I bought for $35 from a dealer in Virginia. I've had it since we moved into our apartment almost twenty years ago. The red iron French café chair, one of a pair that cost $50 each, I bought more recently, at The Little Store in Great Barrington, Massachusetts. To light my work at night, I electrified an old brown bottle (found for $5 at a yard sale) with a lamp-making kit that I got for $7 from a hardware store. The socket is attached to a "stopper"—either a rod wound with thin layers of cork or a knob with flexible plastic fins—that fits snugly into the neck of the bottle. The main disadvantages are that the wire is visible from the top of the neck and that eventually you can count on a little wobbling there. (Electrical tape, wound tightly around the base of the socket, can help alleviate this problem.) Some hardware stores will turn objects into lamps for you and do a more professional-looking job.

Bottom right: In Laurie Warner's studio in Los Angeles (you met her in Western Junk), above her worktable filled with tubes of paint, brushes, colored pencils, and markers, is a nondescript window (if at first you don't see it, look again) transformed by a daring vision and sense of humor. The rather hairlike textured curtains are none other than five dancing hula skirts stretched across the window—three on top, two at the center—café-curtain style. They were 99 cents apiece at Thrifty, an area discount store.

Top left: In front of the brown bottle lamp I made is a bottle in the shape of what we broiled for dinner the night two summers ago when it was given to us. Since I refused to open it (I wanted to save it as a souvenir), we drank red wine with our blue-fish that night. On my desk, it may appear to be—if you'll allow me—a fish out of water, but it comes in handy, just as the other fish, to its left, does, holding down papers from time to time. The cowboy boot next to it, seen serving up pens and pencils, once held a drink in a restaurant in Arizona. The large family gathering in a clay frame decorated with tepees and Native Americans, which came from Room Service in Houston, Texas, for $6, is my own—photographed in 1987. Add three more children and many inches to the little ones present.

Bottom left: Looking a bit like four performers taking a curtain call, these four resin-coated bottles propped in Laurie Warner's studio window were bought at a hospital thrift shop for $1 apiece. They're a gift only a sister could give—and did, to Laurie. "The three on the right I bring out at Christmas and put near the Christmas tree. They remind me of the three Wise Men. I light candles behind them to make them sparkle."

Ellen O'Neill, a collector who believes in "shopping by eye" (as opposed to label or price tag, I presume), and who believes she has "never been into collecting anything valid," has done more than that, all right. (See her apartment and beach house on pages 97–105). Against the cool white tiles of her guest bathroom in New York City, a collection of vintage glass pharmacy bottles, topped with white metal caps, remind her of "a warm and friendly and very hygienic French hospital." She bought them at Wooden Indian in New York City for between $2 and $6 each. The forties "investigative" towel, as Ellen calls it, with the hand-embroidered Sherlock Holmes hat, is the answer to the question it asks. It was for sale in her store, Ellen O'Neill's Supply Store, for $2.50. "No one bought it, so I brought it home." It rests on a cool enamel glazed salt keeper, bought at Brimfield Market in Massachusetts for $24.

In a back corner of Ron Meyer's living room in Los Angeles (see pages 46—47 for other views), what appear to be modern glass sculptures aglow with daylight are in fact five-year-old cast acrylic objects made in Italy, which Ron bought in bulk at an industrial auction in 1989. Eventually, they will become bases for lamps he is designing. (The one peeking out behind them on the table is covered with a very good Victorian rose glass shade.) In the meantime, they continue to mystify guests.

Left: A marbleized yellow-ware tumbler or small vase, with a glazed interior and unglazed exterior, is just the right size to hold unsharpened pencils. I bought it at an antiques shop in Hudson, New York, for $18.

Hating to break up a set, I bought this box of camp craft projects at the Twenty-sixth Street flea market in New York City for $2 each—including the box. Now I display them "as is" on a coffee table at our farm. With the exception of the patchwork one at the top, far right, all are beer bottles. The four rows on the left were marbleized in swirls of paint. The patchwork bottles on the right were made of bits and pieces of masking tape that were then watercolored.

I called a halt to plastic flowers after the arrival of my second swan vase (see following pages for my swan song, so to speak), but then, in November of 1990, just before Thanksgiving, I stopped at 22 Junk-A'Tique on Route 22 in Millerton, New York, and spotted a still life in plastic worthy of Vuillard. Before me, surrounded by plates and glass decanters, was a bouquet of pink roses in a tall thin blue glass vase, reminding me of the work of another artist—Modigliani. Without really thinking of my vow about no more plastic, I bought it for $12.

Above: Ten years ago in Boca Raton, Florida, my husband, Howard, and I celebrated our tenth anniversary at Tom's Place, a restaurant-in-a-trailer known for its home-cooked barbecue and extremely tight quarters. There were six of us squeezed happily at our table, soon filled with heaping plates, and in the center was the sole decorative touch of the restaurant—a plastic swan vase filled with a bouquet of red plastic roses. Why did I fall in love with that thing? I was clearly enchanted with it, and at least one in our group was well aware of that. He spoke to Tom as we departed, and both agreed that my anniversary present that year should not be made of the prescribed material—china—but of plastic! A postscript to the story is that two years ago Howard happened to be back at Tom's for dinner, and this time I got a lavender version of the first swan gift. The two cohabit in my farm atelier (see pages 150–51 for other views) on a dollhouse shelf decorated with a red rose decal that I picked up at the Twenty-sixth Street flea market in New York City for $5.

Right: My "Modigliani" vase with its "Vuillard" bouquet went straight to my heart and then straight to our farmhouse front parlor, where it blooms among other flowers—those on the red-and-white flowered wallpaper behind it and on the chair in the foreground, slipcovered with almost the same pattern, which is mostly obscured by the flowered wool chenille coverlet thrown on it. (For a fuller view, see page 216.) Behind it and to its left are three little parrot prints in bamboo frames. These, the coverlet, and the little parrot oil below, plus the doll's wicker bench it's propped against, all came from the dealer Alice Reid in Livingston, New York, for $12, $35, $8, and $10, respectively. The turtle mirror, flat on its stomach, was $3 at a flea market. The lamp made from a bottle is shaded by an old parchment shade found at a yard sale for 50 cents. The birdhouse leaning in the corner was a Mother's Day present to me from my sons. The lady in pink came from a flea market in London for $20, and the dark print of children playing above it was a couple of dollars at a shop in Red Hook, New York. The still life of peaches to its right has several holes in it—a $4 yard-sale masterpiece.

On the cutting-board counter that separates her kitchen from her dining room, Grace Coddington—an Englishwoman in New York City (see pages 168–171 for more)—has filled her artifact-encrusted vase with a brilliant bouquet of tulips. She bought it for $100 at Kelter-Malcé, a landmark shop in Greenwich Village in New York City. According to the shop owners, who discovered it in Pennsylvania, it is a memory jar from no later than the 1930s. "What it's about," they say, "is personal memorabilia"—things no longer useful but personally meaningful to the maker, like a doll's head, a half of a locket, stray buttons, and shards of glass or crockery saved by pressing them in a puttylike substance that then dried. The result is a one-of-a-kind 3-D scrapbook. "There's lots of lore attached to memory jars," reports Jerry Harmyk, a collector and the creator of U.S.E.D. and Kitschen, two other Greenwich Village shops specializing in American collectibles. "Though they eventually became a form of craft, originally in the Deep South, they were created not only to save the personal small artifacts of a recently departed loved one but, more important, to seal in his or her spirit. In some places, particularly in Louisiana, they can still be seen on top of graves." (See an example of a memory jar on page 22.)

Above: This past Christmas I decided it would be festive to stack red books around a small Christmas tree we keep on a table in our farmhouse front parlor (the same room seen on the previous pages). The books, collected from bookstores and flea markets here and abroad, cover everything from dogs to bee-keeping and cost from 25 cents to $25. After the tree was put away, the red books stayed (they added such cheer to the room), and a funny red, green, and gold painted glass vase with protruding grape clusters took the place of the tree. My sister Liza found the vase—with enamel roses in place—for $2 at The Rummage Shoppe on Route 22 in Millerton, New York, and (with a little friendly persuasion) left it as a weekend present. According to Kevin de Martine, a bottle collector and proprietor of a bottle and antiques shop nearby, it's a pickle jar made of Goofus glass. Though primarily used for carnival prizes (see the plates on page 55), Goofus glass was used for a variety of objects sold in general and department stores. What started as a hot trend around 1890 died by 1920. Owners were disappointed with the way the paint—mostly reds and greens on grounds of metallic gold or bronze—held up (it didn't!), which probably explains the poor paint job done by a former owner attempting to restore the jar's original colors.

Left: Another Goofus glass pickle jar, found at a tag sale for $1, has lost all its original paint except for scant flecks of gold and burgundy. This is probably the condition the jar above was in before it was repainted.

O f all the things Ron Meyer—an artist and designer of textiles, clothes, and, most recently, "romantic" nightclub interiors—has created, it is perhaps his own home, a little bougainvillea-wrapped thirties bungalow on a busy street in Los Angeles (seen at top), that is his best and most personal accomplishment. The first thing Ron did after a move from San Francisco in 1986 was to buy the house and immediately plant two lantana bushes between it and the street. By the end of the second year, the front of the house was totally hidden. The driveway that originally led to a garage stops at a gate, which leads to the house's new entrance (see above), marked by French folding doors and an enthusiastic greeter—Harry, Ron's eight-year-old border collie (seen at right).

Left: Harry sits at attention in front of a portrait of Rupert Everett, the English actor, painted in 1984 by Ron. "It was a total fantasy," as is the French two-tiered table below the portrait, which Ron got at an auction for $50 and decorated with several art glass pieces from his collection. One of his favorites, the red piece on top filled with limes, came from a flea market in Long Beach, California, and was a gift from his mother. It was part of a set of three primitive hand-blown art glass pieces from the 1930s or 1940s. The Venetian glass ashtray to the left of it is from a large collection Ron's gathered at flea markets and auctions. "In the last two years Venetian glass has become very trendy," Ron says with a sigh. "This ashtray that cost ten dollars then probably costs eighty today." The grape compote below is one piece—an Italian porcelain from the fifties, bought at an auction for around $20. To the left is an Italian cast-glass table lighter from the fifties, and to the right is a cast-glass English lidded sweets dish from the twenties, found at a flea market for $10.

Above: Along the red windowsill of Ron's living-room window is a convention of glass pieces representing Ron's eclectic taste. At the right is a cherry-colored Venetian glass ashtray from the 1960s, picked up for $20 at Abell's Auction Company in Commerce, a suburb of Los Angeles. A Vaseline-glass candy dish from the twenties was picked up for $40.

The centerpiece of the collection—"actually, the best piece I own," says Ron—is the tall Murano glass vase from Venice, holding a bouquet of handmade glass flowers. The vase was a bargain for $100 at Butterfield's auction house in L.A. The posies came from the Rose Bowl flea market for $35.

"The enamel vase I found at a flea market in Lyon and had it fitted for a client, and then changed my mind," Ron admits. The nineteenth-century English glass candlestick is one of a pair bought for $100 at Abell's. The pale yellow bud vase, bought by Ron's assistant, Sabryna, in 1989 at the glass factory in Murano, Italy, was presented to him on her first day of work.

A pair of pressed-glass compotes and a bud vase cost no more than a dollar or two apiece at a tag sale in Copake, New York. The one at left displays a collection of swizzle sticks I bought for a total of $7. Behind them is a $2 paint-by-numbers tulip painting and a headless lady, bought for $12 from a junk shop in upstate New York. The pickle-handled salad spoon was a quarter from a junk shop in San Francisco.

solid gold

SEARCH FOR
SATURDAY, July 27th

· American Flag stuff - red, white & blue stuff

· gold stuff

· kitchen stuff
· glittery stuff?
· blk & white
· carnival
· under 25¢ - under $1.00
· linen sheets

In the fields of junk, all that glitters is not gold. Most of what gold diggers turn up is likely to be brass, copper, or, more often than not, gold paint. The real value is in hitting the mother lode when you least expect it, or enjoying the humor of exhibiting glitzy stuff in unlikely surroundings. Consider, for example, Robert Miller's "golden" fruit salad on the opposite page, bottom row, tossed with a prized golden pineapple tray, a gilded lily pad, and a trio of golden apples. The heroic charioteers above it, seen on pages 56–57, and installed in a make-believe hayloft palace, were bought off the curb at a used-furniture store in upstate New York. Miriam Wosk, a Los Angeles artist, Midas-touched a primitive twig table with gold paint (see page 59) and encrusted the top with jewels to live in her Frank Gehry home of white walls and glass. When I spotted the pair of golden glass plates, seen opposite, top row, asked the owners what they were made of, and was told "Goofus glass"—carnival prizes of the early twentieth century—my gold rush began. As evidence, scan my crumpled list, seen opposite, top left. Making a list before a day of foraging is like having a map of your own treasure hunt and gives you an answer when a dealer asks, "Are you looking for something specific?" "Well, as a matter of fact, yes. Do you have anything in gold?" What success! There were wall plaques, a horseshoe, candelabra, Cinderella's slipper, a china collection, ashtrays and bowls, glass vases, Christmas ornaments, cowboy hats, salad bowls, and picture frames. My treasures, laid out on the previous pages, cost less than $10 total! Indiana Jones, eat your heart out!

Previous pages: A scavenger hunt for (fool's) gold at a large outdoor flea market produced, left to right, a collection of brass wall plaques (seen later on pages 56–57), a golden horseshoe, a slightly crooked candelabrum, a leather jewelry box under Cinderella's slipper, a fragile demitasse and saucer, an ashtray, a gold-and-white striped glass vase from the fifties, a Christmas-tree warbler, a golden straw cowboy hat, a stack of shining salad bowls, and a stack of useful picture frames. Total retail value? $7.50.

Opposite page, clockwise from top left: A forager's list; a pair of Goofus glass plates displayed at the Twenty-sixth Street flea market in New York City; assorted flea-market booty; a brass tureen shining amid tag-sale clutter; a golden fruit salad; a pair of powdered and wigged figures riding home in a truck; and golden charioteers in bas-relief.

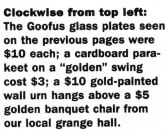

Clockwise from top left:
The Goofus glass plates seen
on the previous pages were
$10 each; a cardboard para-
keet on a "golden" swing
cost $3; a $10 gold-painted
wall urn hangs above a $5
golden banquet chair from
our local grange hall.

Our old wooden carriage house in upstate New York is transformed, in summer, from a garage for our truck to an open-air game room. A Ping Pong table is set up opposite the main viewing stand, left, a grain-painted church pew, which I bid $35 for at an auction. Beneath it resides a phalanx of galvanized tin water cans collected at flea markets and tag sales for $5 total. The message on the pink (presumably once-red) fire bucket on the bamboo table reads "For Fire Only." It cost $15. The pennants hanging below were bought for $1. The metal kitchen stools to either side, dragged in for play-off seating, cost $5 apiece. The shelves on the back wall, crammed with motor oil, jars of nails, car wax, and spray paint, recently made room for more "golden" kinds of clutter. Side by side, they begin to resemble the dioramas of the artist Joseph Cornell.

Above: Up the paint-spattered staircase, seen on the previous pages, in a huge loft where hay was once stacked, lies a wasteland of white space devoted, at present, to not much more than a long wooden table (seen at right) and another gold mine (of sorts)—a collection of shiny, hammered brass wall plaques depicting scenes of medieval courting and carousing, ships at sea, and skaters waltzing, mostly from the fifties. Their roots can be traced back to the walls of European pubs, gaming rooms, and libraries of the seventeenth century. Today, they're a guaranteed find at almost any yard sale or flea-market stand. I started collecting them at a quarter each, thinking they would add a certain wayward glamour to the summer eating hall we're planning for this upstairs space. The inspiration was an old drafty hall I once saw in an English castle, complete with trestle table, long benches, and chandeliers hanging from the rafters, candlelight from which was reflected in the real golden chargers sitting on shelves on the wall. Our dream is incomplete, but growing.

Left: A golden bas-relief, found in a used-furniture store in Amenia, New York, measures a healthy 39″ × 23″. The subject is classical, the result is not. Made of some kind of waxlike synthetic poured into a mold, then painted with silver and gold leaf (or something that resembles them), it was a bargain at $45. A white sheet, thrown over an old bench below it, resembles a cast-off toga from the charioteers above.

miriam Wosk is an artist whose vision is inspired by things she collects—screens and furniture, patterned textiles, sequins and glitter. Some of these ("many of these," she confirms) inspirations were foraged from flea markets. Often, they're gold. The French Art Deco gold-leaf dressing table, seen at right in her Los Angeles bedroom, was bought not at a flea market but from a dealer on Melrose Avenue. The turn-of-the-century headless gilt display mannequin exhibited on its left and, close up, on the opposite page was bought at the first exhibit of modernist art and furniture she attended in New York City seven or eight years ago. She paid about $400 for it. "I saw it as a great sculptural form." Her display of Bakelite bracelets stacked on paint rollers (seen at right and on the opposite page) have been her mix-and-match signature for more than ten years. "I collected them when they were still affordable." The same goes for the plastic necklaces hung around the mannequin's neck—"all bought from antique shows and fairs. I never spent more than twenty to twenty-five dollars for them." The painted woman's head to the left, a display piece from the 1930s, has been Miriam's so long she doesn't even remember where she got it. The ringleted ceramic woman on the right is actually a flower vase given to her by a friend who knew of her fondness for heads and faces.

Above: "I've always decorated anything I could get my hands on: chairs, lamps, curtains, pillows, ceramics, boots," Miriam admitted in a recent interview. Case in point: the Adirondack-style bent twig table she bought, then tucked away, "because it was too rustic" for her very modern, very white new quarters. Later, she had a vision and transformed it into "a luxe object" by gold-leafing it and resurfacing the top with faux pearls and junk jewels. The Midas touch? Unquestionably!

Above and right: Another corner of Miriam Wosk's bedroom reveals what appears to be a miniature staircase from a Busby Berkley musical. "Not far off," Miriam agrees. She had it created to showcase a chorus line of bronze statuettes (some gilt, some silvered) assembled over the course of twenty-five years. "I love their Amazon strength and athletic poses." Some came from the legendary Marche aux Puces Clignancourt in Paris and flea markets in London, Los Angeles, and New York. "They're not the greatest. They were mass-produced in the twenties and thirties. I paid twenty to thirty dollars for them. But when you see things in repetition, they seem better!" (For more of Miriam Wosk's collected "repetitions," see pages 94–95.)

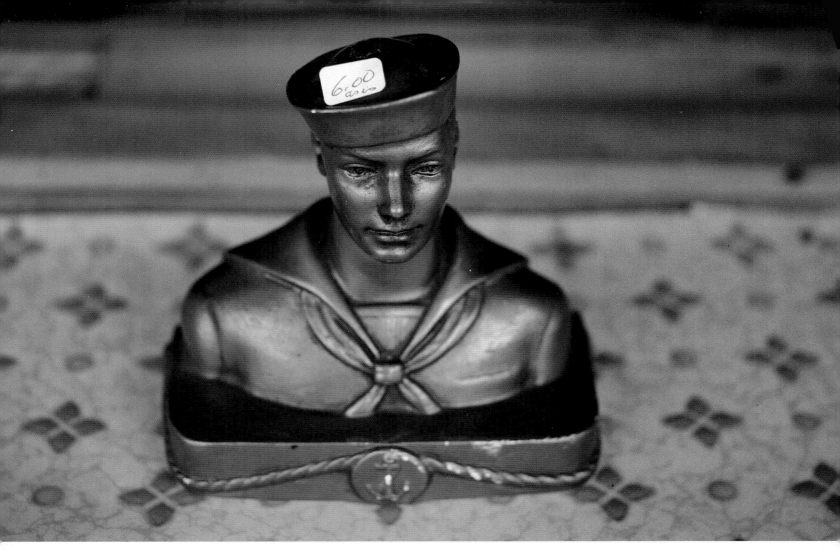

Above: A plaster sailor found at a roadside tag sale in upstate New York looks to have fallen into the clutches of Goldfinger. Probably a carnival prize or bookend, it cost, as the sticker attests, "$6.00 as is." The "as is," not seen in the picture, refers to a hefty chunk missing under his chin.

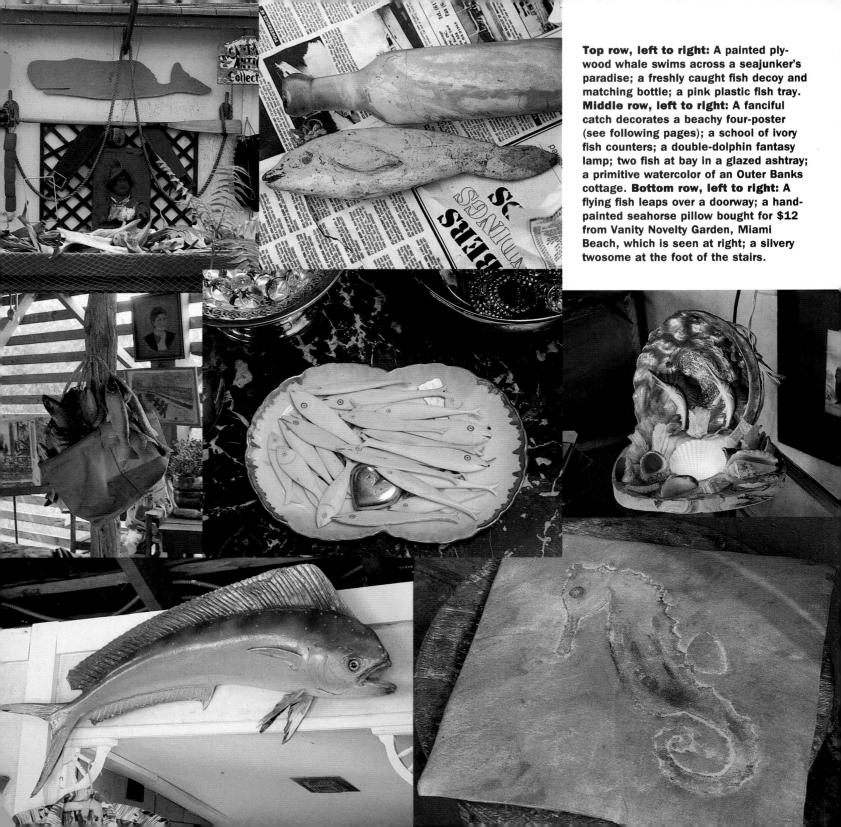

Top row, left to right: A painted plywood whale swims across a seajunker's paradise; a freshly caught fish decoy and matching bottle; a pink plastic fish tray. **Middle row, left to right:** A fanciful catch decorates a beachy four-poster (see following pages); a school of ivory fish counters; a double-dolphin fantasy lamp; two fish at bay in a glazed ashtray; a primitive watercolor of an Outer Banks cottage. **Bottom row, left to right:** A flying fish leaps over a doorway; a hand-painted seahorse pillow bought for $12 from Vanity Novelty Garden, Miami Beach, which is seen at right; a silvery twosome at the foot of the stairs.

Start with the fish decoys on the preceding pages, carved up so cleverly by the North Carolina artist Charles Reber, add the wide variety of fishy forms swimming loose on these pages, and you begin to catch the spirit of why it's sometimes fun to throw your line into the sea of junk and get hooked on one kind of theme. All the collectors on the following pages (not a Pisces among them!) have something fishy in their homes, apartments, bedrooms, beach houses, kitchens, and consciousnesses.

Previous pages: The catch of the day, provided by the handiwork and wit of Charles Reber, an almost legendary wood-carver of the Outer Banks of North Carolina. In the summer of 1991, his hand-carved and -painted fish decoys ranged in price from $20 for a weighted 8-inch ice fish (see the green one next to the candy can) to $2 for the natural, unpainted cutout below it.

In most coastline communities, where shifting sands and high tides are the rule, beach houses are built on pilings or stilts. Some owners board up the sides of the space under the house and lay a concrete floor to make a garage or outdoor shower. Few, however, have thought to create an open-air bedroom like the one at left. The team—my mother, father, several of my sisters, and me—took off for yard sales, junk and thrift shops, and, one night, an auction. The bed was built from fishermen's trap stakes, found on the beach and wedged under the rather low ceiling. A mattress was laid over cinder blocks, and two large flags, bought at the auction for $10 apiece, were chosen as headboard and bedspread. A fishnet was chosen as a seaworthy bed ruffle. As things progressed, the anticipated guest seemed clear—either Neptune's bride or a bohemian artist, not unlike the exotic Frida Kahlo. The total spent was less than $100. The chair above, for example, cost $1.30, the painting $8. Every beach house, especially a rental, needs a little personalization. For a week or two, why not be outrageous?

The beautiful flag (country unknown) at the head of the bed was chosen at auction for its astonishing size, sea-foamy colors, and the regal bird with the world's longest tail feathers. It and five others, including the red one laid over the bed, were flying from the auction's entrance until our scavenger team made a bid of $10 each for them. The floral pillow was borrowed from an unsuspecting family member's bed.

If the above was a scratch-and-sniff picture, you'd smell nothing amiss. Bought in New York City, this catch is fragrance free. Now, it entertains hordes of visiting children. The fishnet dust ruffle was once a prop in a local seafood restaurant. The rug on the plywood floor is a $2 beach mat.

The members of the team that brought this clock from a junk lot dubbed it the "Jell-O Rock Clock," obviously not what the makers intended. It cost $12 and now, after its summer stint, keeps perfect time on an eighteenth-century mahogany sideboard in a charming (but slightly eclectic) apartment in New York City.

For bedside viewings, a still life found on sale in a barn in upstate New York for about $20 was lent by my mother. It was a summer housewarming gift from my sister, who was captivated by its Matisse-at-Nice sensibility. The blue music stand was found during rounds at a junk shop for $10.

Judyth vanAmringe, a New York City artist, collector, and shopkeeper of the unusual (more on pages 132–33 and 136–137), is a fisher of all things bright and shiny. If they happen to be fish, well, even better! The leader of her school of five was caught at a flea market in Barcelona several years back for $50. "These are not Venetian glass works of art," she states. "They're made in Czechoslovakia, Spain, Italy—all over. You can even find them in Miami. For me they're just pretty souvenirs."

In the front hall of Doug Taylor's bed-and-breakfast in Guilford, New York (see pages 24–27), you are greeted by the accoutrements of a certain kind of sporting visitor. Dropped—in haste, you gather—on the needlepoint seat of the most formal kind of Queen Anne chair (one of a set of eight bought by Doug for $100, from an ad in the <u>PennySaver</u>*) is a very handsome fishing creel draped with the most arresting collection of lures, each more colorful and exotic than the next. Flung over the back of the chair is a red wool jacket stitched to the hilt with what appear to be Boy Scout jamboree patches. You consider a very early breakfast to catch a glimpse of what in your imagination is a Hemingway-esque-giant-of-a-sportsman/adventurer, when Doug explains that the creel is a souvenir of his "pond life" collecting days. "The embossed fish buckle and handsome leather strap really turned me on." It had, before this, hung in a "pond life" bathroom he had put together. The lures, it seems, belonged to his dad, "a really good fisherman." Doug bought the jacket—"Yes, those are Boy Scout jamboree patches"—for $15, when he was into his "camping junk" phase. Moral: Let sleeping lures lie!

* The <u>PennySaver</u> is one of the many weekly free community papers that are published throughout the United States. If you are not receiving one and want to know if one exists in your area, you may contact your local Chamber of Commerce or the national Association of Free Community Papers at (312) 644-6610.

Above: A recent 25-cent catch made by Doug Taylor is this Hawaiian butterfly angelfish. "At first I thought it was a plastic pocketbook," Doug offers, "but, upon closer examination, I determined that it's a plant hanger. It is probably from the fifties, and was designed to hang in one of those aquatically themed bathrooms." Doug's nature knowledge is impressive; he once owned ninety aquariums! "My friends laughingly call me Deep End. I do tend to go overboard on things!" The wooden stool was found by a friend on a street in New York City. Though you can't see them here, each leg is painted a different color.

Sharone Einhorn, the mistress of the turreted Cape Cod house glimpsed at left, is also the co-owner of an antiques shop not more than ten miles away. She is a little hesitant to speak of how much she paid for the two fish lithographs, far left and above, circa 1880.

"Well, if you really must know . . . They were eight dollars for the pair."

"With the beautiful old frames?" I persist.

"Yes, I'm afraid so," she admits. "I got them so cheap," she continues, "because they were crumbling. They came from the attic of an old house."

"And what about the beautiful bedspread?"

"That came from another house sale, in East Hampton. There were a pair. Toile de Jouy; they cost sixty-five dollars."

"And the little clock on the table?"

"Well, it's just a clock case. I found it at a yard sale. No, I can't tell you the price! It was," she says, faltering, "fifty cents!"

the little cypress house below, called Duck House by its owners, has been weathering in the sun and salt air on the Outer Banks of North Carolina for almost a century. The penthouse studio on the opposite page, perched like an elegant fishing shack fifteen stories up in New York City, has been there half as long. Both boast water views—of Currituck Sound and the Hudson River, respectively. Both have portholes. The one in Duck, seen at right, is mainly ornamental, salvaged from an old ship sunk in nearby waters. The urban version, seen at the far right, is functional, cut into an outer wall by its visionary owner, Richard Giglio, who transformed the dingy three-room apartment into a spare, shipshape cabin.

Below and right: On the back porch of Duck House, a weathered wall exhibits seaworthy finds: from the top, a $12 wooden fish head, a dangling porthole, a trio of Styrofoam floats (past their prime) found on the beach, and a bucket of Outer Banks birds, $12 each.

Top and left: After the tar roof of his urban aerie was planked and the exterior walls were sided, Richard Giglio started a windproof garden. Five years later, a hardy array of cedars, ornamental grasses, sunflowers, morning glories, marigolds, Russian sage, and "only the scruffiest kinds of roses" make Richard seem like the kind of gardener even Jack of beanstalk fame could trust.

Middle and above: On the other side of the porthole, aground in the tangled undergrowth of a spidery aloe plant and an albino palm tree made of paper, is a small boat bound from Key West, made of matchsticks by prison inmates.

Right and below: When Richard Giglio moved into his New York home, he brought with him only what was "essential," like the Louis XV chair, seen at top right. "It's the granddaddy of the apartment. I've always had it. The pillow in its lap was something someone wanted to throw away!" Also essential was the round brass Moroccan Art Deco table picked up in a New York shop for $100. "Junk is affordable. I've never bought anything I couldn't pay for on the spot!" The pair of Limoges maroon and silver bowls, one of which is seen below holding star fruit and nectarines, was a gift from an old friend, for whom the bowls were made in Paris, in 1928. They are seen as stove-top decor at right, along with a sailboat model (seen close up at top) Richard found in Key West for "very little." The rusty air vent directly above the sink, another Key West discovery, reminds Richard of a Brancusi sculpture—"not bad for one dollar." (For more details on this shelf, see following pages.)

Left and below: The fact is, everything in Richard Giglio's apartment is "essential"—like the leaning tower of old art books and magazines, topped with shells like gobs of whipped cream and nuts on ice-cream sundaes. Or the little paper-and-wood lantern next to them, from a Japanese department store. Or, in front of it, the classic bronze of Psyche, found at a Paris flea market for $20. At the bottom, postcards of Matisse and other subjects, shells, Japanese cooking utensils, and a beautiful (expensive) Venetian mirror—they're all essential. Because Richard Giglio sees them as elements in the collages and paintings he creates, "when one element is moved or changed, so is the effect. The secret to buying junk," sums up Richard, "is to buy or find what appeals to you without a specific place for the object in mind." And food for thought: "Everything eventually becomes junk!"

Following pages: Richard Giglio is an artist who prefers paper to canvas and thumbtacks to frames. Key West, his second home, seems especially evident in this Sea World-meets-Matisse kind of still life on the shelf above his kitchen sink. The pair of straw fish ("probably from Taiwan, probably worth $3") were "inherited." The globe, "from the best thrift shop in New York City, gone now," cost $1. The rare painting of Versailles on metal, glimpsed to the right, was a gift. The ship's lantern came from a clothing shop in Key West.

Monet at Giverny

THE
HORIZON
BOOK
OF THE

ARTS O

JU

kitchen junk

Clockwise from top left: Krims Krams, in San Francisco, was a "quality" resource for two kitchen finds—salt and pepper shakers and pottery bowls—seen in my carriage-house atelier on page 92. To the right, a tag-sale cache of glasses is for sale for a quarter and up in upstate New York. To their right, this whole box went for less than $5 at a thrift shop in San Francisco. To the right, wooden-handled utensils like these were popular in the forties. At right, a flowery pitcher goes for a special price at a roadside tag sale on Route 22 in upstate New York. Below it, a trio of kitchen canisters refurbished with paint and decals costs $5. Below left, the green wooden napkin holder shaped like a teapot, seen on page 90–91, is from Pink Paraffin in San Francisco. To its right, the two yellow pottery bowls discovered at Krims Krams can also be seen on top of my cupboard on page 92. Below, kitchen utensils take on a surreal air in the windows at Cookin' in San Francisco. To the left, the stack-up of metal bread boxes are also from Cookin'. Above the boxes are pottery fruits and vegetables from Praiseworthy Antiques in Guilford, New York. To the left of the bread boxes—their home, Cookin' in San Francisco. To the left are bushel baskets of values at Fishs Eddy in New York City. Above them, at Cookin', are shelves of orange-juice squeezers looking like an army of the little robot of <u>Star Wars</u> fame—"R2D2."

Survey the kitchen gizmos, tabletop bric-a-brac, storage bins, and utensils seen at left and you begin to understand the attraction they hold not only for serious cooks but for anyone seeking to liven up the room (aside from the bedroom) that we live in the most. While more utilitarian-minded collectors search out the kind of recycled gourmet appurtenances that are the specialty of shops like Cookin', in San Francisco, and Kitschen, in New York City, others, like collectors of vintage Fiesta Ware, shop solely with an eye for shape and color. A table set with old linens, mix-and-match china, glassware, flatware, and condiment holders is not only economically viable but downright appetizing. Though the Cuisinart may have been the kitchen tool of the eighties, most of the collectors on the pages to come probably passed on it for an old cutting board and a chopper.

Previous pages: Leave it to an acclaimed graphic artist (and obsessive collector), namely Robert Miles Runyon, who resides in Manhattan Beach, California (for more of his collections, see page 116), to turn a perfectly functional old Globe stove into a showcase for a gourmet collector's feast of kitchen tins, crockery, and a chicken in an old enamel pot.

Right: It was in 1983 in a crowded shop in San Francisco that Ron Meyer, an artist and interior decorator, came across this rather surreal painting of a housewife, which cost $10. Since then, she has followed Ron from his kitchen in San Francisco to the kitchen she dominates in his present home in Los Angeles. (For more on Meyer's collections, see pages 37 and 46—47.) "At first, looking at the style of her kitchen, I thought she was from the thirties, but then," he points out, "she wouldn't have had the TV," which is what ultimately saves her from the drudgery of her chores. Raising her plate as she would a large castanet, she stars in her own musical fantasy, backed up by the chorus of dancers she watches on her breadbox-sized, black-and-white TV screen.

Far right: In our carriage house in New York State, a large tabby cat (in a poster of a lithograph by Nathaniel Cullerson) keeps constant surveillance over a screened pie safe filled with kitchen gadgets and household equipment, mostly from the twenties. His shift seems endless, timed by the alarm clock under his nose, which was bought for its purity of design (a dollar's worth!) rather than its function. The lineup of graters and flour sifters on the top shelf cost an average of $8 apiece. The child's tin stove, from Germany, cost ten times that, but was hard to resist, outfitted as it was with its own tiny utensils and cookware. The baking molds for lady fingers lining the second shelf cost $3 and $4 and have lost their usefulness only in <u>my</u> hands, since I am not a baker. The orange-juice-glass pitchers, collected for their stripes, were $5 to $6 apiece. The green enamel bowl, $10, is filled with silverplated forks and spoons, bought for $20. It was found, along with the set of six (three are inside the others) blue plaid canisters below, at Cookin', a kitchen store in San Francisco, which specializes in, according to its sign (seen on the preceding pages), "recycled gourmet appurtenances." The odd utensils scattered around came from Big John's, an odds-and-ends store also in San Francisco. The green wooden box and tin painting above it were local tag-sale pickups for a couple of dollars.

Rescuing Old Flatware

When buying old flatware for the table, keep in mind that stains and rust are very often immovable. For rust, Judy Kaminsky of Cookin', in San Francisco, suggests dipping a piece of very fine steel wool in cooking oil and rubbing lightly. Mary Levenstein and Cordelia Biddle, authors of Caring for Your Cherished Possessions, advise polishing silver as little as possible, and, when necessary, using the purest, mildest product available, such as calcium carbonate mixed with olive oil (which is nontoxic and can be cleaned off when dry) or Goddard's silver polish. Judy Kaminsky takes a more practical stance, suggesting most commercial polishes are fine so long as their use is followed up with a good soap-and-water washing. On intricately worked silver, Levenstein and Biddle suggest you get to the rough spots with the softest available natural-bristle toothbrush. Do not wrap silver in felt, chamois, or newspaper. The first two are sources of hydrogen sulfide, a heavy-duty tarnisher, and the printer's ink in the newspaper will eventually remove the plating.

Top left: On a counter in Grace Coddington's kitchen in New York City (see page 44 for more), a porcelain pitcher spouts a harmonious mix of old and new utensils. The onlooker behind and to the right is a wooden-pig cutting board. The brown crock to the left is a receptacle for chopsticks.

Top right: Tag-sale knives, badly rusted or tarnished, can be cleaned up, machine buffed, or replated. I buy them just for the look of the handles—certainly worth it if the price is as seen on the stickers!

I love old flatware, particularly styles with bone, wooden, or some form of cel-
luloid handles. I mix them together—silver, silverplate, coin silver, stainless
steel, and even tin—and set my table that way. I loved the blue Bakelite handles on the fifteen-piece fish set seen here at the Twenty-Sixth Street flea
market in New York City. The damaged handles didn't bother me. The price—
$60—did.

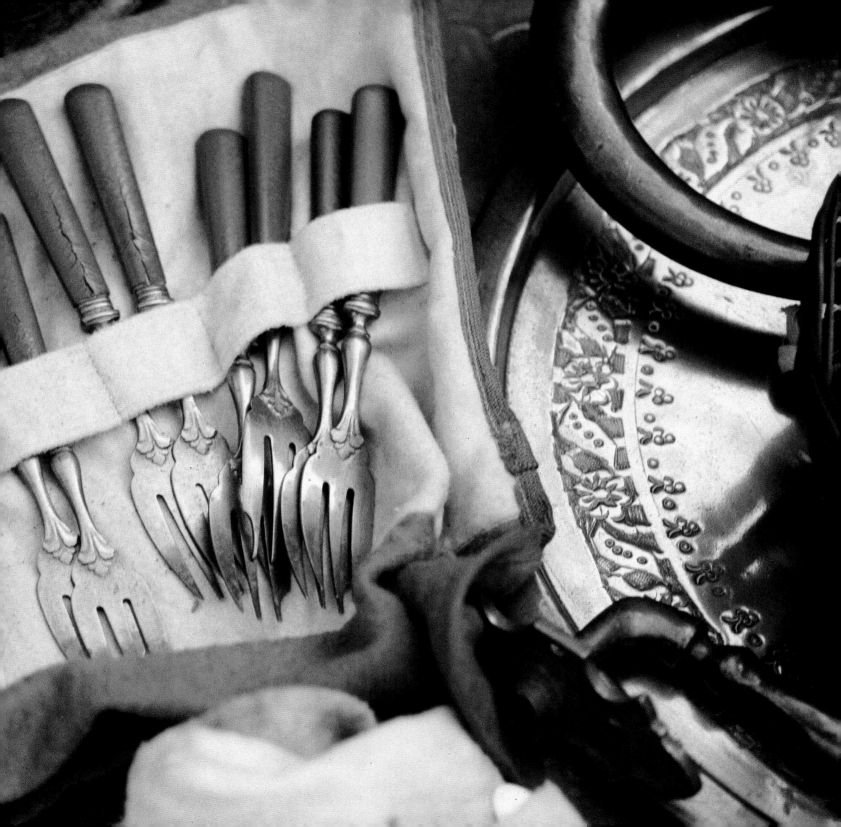

Top and above: A summer tag sale goes alfresco on the grounds of the Copake Country Auction house in Copake, New York, where these fresh-picked strawberry pots and flowery table linens were found.

Left: A tag-sale tea party set up on our farmhouse porch. Everything, except the lilacs and doughnuts, was scavenged out of tag-sale boxes from New York to California. The whole spread cost $93.50.

TAG-SALE TEA-PARTY TALLY

Tablecloth	$ 2.00
2 Napkins	.50
Strawberry teapot	2.00
Strawberry cachepot	2.50
Green wooden napkin holder in the shape of a teapot	20.00
3 Pastel-rimmed plates	.75
3 Flowered dessert plates	3.00
Blue doughnut tray	2.00
2 Blue enamel spoons	4.00
2 Tea-bag holders	3.00
Salt and pepper shakers	13.00
Blue dog	1.00
2 Tea mugs	1.00
Red-cow creamer	1.00
Table	35.00
9 Doughnuts	2.50
2 Tea bags	.25
Total:	**$93.50**

Above: Dig deeply into tag-sale boxes of old linens, and you'll be rewarded, as I was, with the likes of this trio of hand-embroidered dish towels for a quarter apiece. Use them for drying dishes, in your bathroom for guests, at your dinner table as luxurious napkins, or do as Miriam Wosk does and make them into pillow cases or sofa covers (seen at far right).

Right: In our carriage-house atelier in upstate New York, the bold colors of Gauguin's Tahitian women—a framed reproduction that cost $5—are picked up in the more common kitchen accessories below them. From left, dozens of plastic swizzle sticks stuck in a storage container came "as is" from a San Francisco thrift shop for $5 (see also pages 48–49). The pair of pottery bowls, originally from Mexico and also found in San Francisco, were $2. Stacked under the Polynesian apples is a set of metal picnic plates. All six cost $48. The enamel bowls to the right were collected from the same place—Cookin', in San Francisco—for $6 each. The fruits-and-nuts still life above them was $8 at a shop in Richmond, Virginia. Above it, a collection of tin picnic baskets and lunch pails, plus a peeling red milk cooler, was picked up from all over. Stored in the old screened cupboard below (which I took possession of for a $10 bid at a country auction) are assorted salt and pepper shakers, small enamel cook pots, and illustrated children's tin and plastic plates. Folded below are slightly untidy tablecloths, dish towels, and napkins, brightly patterned like the native pareus wrapped around the young Polynesians above them.

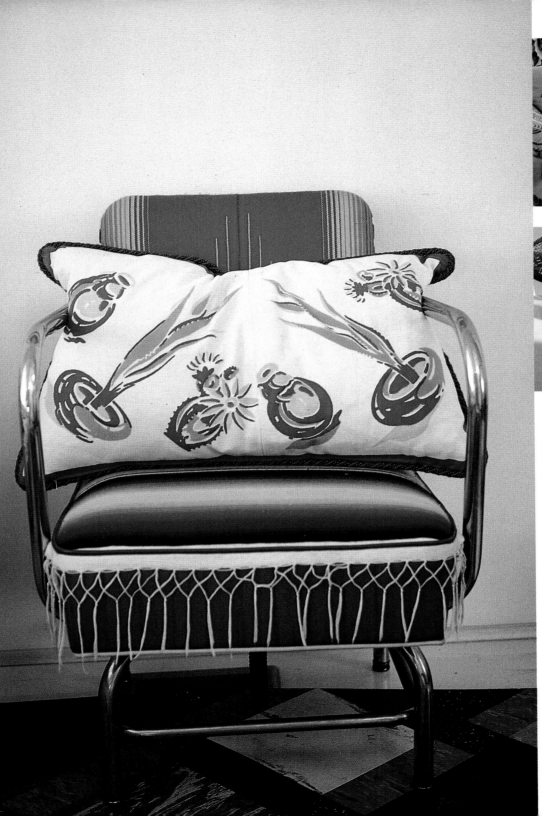

Left: When Miriam Wosk, a Los Angeles artist and furniture designer (see pages 58–60), commissioned architect Frank Gehry to redesign a house she bought ten years ago in Beverly Hills, one of the first things she bought was an old chrome chair from the thirties, upholstered with a fringed and striped wool serape. "The mix frightened me," admits Miriam, "but somehow it really worked together." The pillow, made out of a Mexican dish towel—part of a large collection—came later.

Top: Some of Miriam's favorite red-white-and-blue kitchen towels and tablecloths (collected over ten years for $3 to $5 and $12 to $15, respectively) were donated to the redo of a living-room sofa. She combined them with new mattress-type ticking.

Above: Not far from the chrome chair and kitchen-towel sofa is another lively vintage dish towel, featuring a Spanish dancer. Draped near a mirrored mosaic table by the artist Dan Biler, and a chair by Miriam, it raises the question "Can a new pillow be far off?"

Top left: In front of an FDR tray found in a shop in Venice, California, is a pitcher in the shape of a woman's face—"if Salvador Dali had designed kitchenware, I'd swear he had done this," says Miriam. Lined up next to the pitcher at right is a ceramic pig put to work storing small utensils, a stack of Fiesta Ware bowls (the lidded versions are hard to come by), a clown jar, and a majolica sunflower pitcher filled with assorted salad servers. The tray behind it is a souvenir from Rio de Janeiro made from butterfly wings, which cost $40 at a New York antiques show twenty years ago. The two metal serving trays in front are from the thirties—picked up for about $20.

Top right: A window-ledge collection of ceramic creamers arranged in descending pecking order was innocently hatched with one Miriam found at a flea market. "I found another pair and before I knew it I had a flock! They don't go south in winter." Sometimes collecting is like eating popcorn.

miriam Wosk loves her kitchen. She says, "It's the energy center of our home," shared with her husband, Steve, and five-year-old son, Adam. Fueled by the colors of Fiesta Ware—that inexpensive machine-manufactured tabletop line from the thirties and forties, and recently reintroduced—old California pottery, "especially Malibu ceramics," and the rich visual heritage of Mexico, "my kitchen has been described," Miriam admits, "as an Aztec deco temple."

Right: The roots of Miriam Wosk's collecting began in New York City about twenty-five years ago, when a good friend with a good eye and a shop of his own took her to her first flea market. "I probably picked up my first Fiesta Ware pitcher that day. I was attracted by their intense colors and the shapes." Fifteen years' worth of that obsession lines seven shelves in Miriam's sunny dining-room nook. Miriam collected each pitcher, one at a time, for approximately $8 or $10. A special few went for as high as $50. Many came from the Rose Bowl swap meet in Pasadena.

Middle left: On the shelf above the corrugated stainless-steel bar is a lineup of celebrity cookie jars—from Howdy Doody to Pinocchio—representing fourteen years of focused searching. "Mostly I paid around twenty-five or thirty dollars for them," says Miriam.

Bottom left and far left: A stack of Fiesta Ware plates and bowls collected over a twenty-year period for an average price of $15 apiece, a glassware set that cost $12 per glass, a polka-dotted pitcher from the forties (a wedding present), and Bakelite-handled stainless-steel flatware picked up in Sun Valley, Idaho, for $150 are overseen by a ceramic vase of Carmen Miranda (collected fifteen years ago for $60).

In Ohio, not the state but a small, lively shop located in Venice, California, owned and run by Carol Hillman (who hails from, not surprisingly, Poland, Ohio), furniture from the thirties, forties, and fifties spills out the front door onto the street. If you take the time to wind your way through it, you will find, halfway back, an old cupboard (seen at right) filled with put-out-to-pasture kitchen equipment from as far back as the turn of the century, recalling those pre-high-tech days in the kitchen when housewifery took forever. In 1919, Lydia Ray Balderston, an instructor at Teachers College, Columbia University, taught a course in it—Housewifery and Laundering—and wrote a Lippincott Home Manual entitled, simply, House-wifery. "The poetry of life always has a practical side to it and most practical affairs rightly worked out are full of poetry," she wrote. Some of the tools of yesteryear's kitchens intrigue us for their ingenuity, design, and sentimental value, but some, like the enamel pots and the custard cups at right (which I bought for $8), are even, after all these years, "darn useful," as Carol Hillman puts it. And they possibly bring with them something of what Ms. Balderston was getting at: summer corn boiling in a white enamel pot—is that not poetry?

Left: Every teenage girl needs a dressing table. Bridget O'Neill, daughter of Ellen O'Neill (of whom we'll learn more in the next few pages), is no different. What is different is <u>what</u> her mother came up with. Not the old beveled glass mirror, for which she paid $8, or the old faded rosebud fabric from the forties, which Ellen cleverly stapled to the front of the table, but certainly the metal high chair in front of it, obviously meant for a kitchen or an old-fashioned dental clinic, bought in Pennsylvania for $12, and, without question, the step-on-the-pedal fifties trash can, complete with fruit decal, which Ellen bought for $14. "I love metal and tin kitchen elements in the bedroom," states Ellen emphatically. "That little metal chair is very comfortable—a kitchen doesn't give it meaning! And the trash basket—how convenient for Bridget to just push her foot down! And I love the way the decal works with the rosebud skirt above it." The chipped china dogs were collected by Bridget. The tin plaid picnic basket stores supplies for Bridget's desk, which this table doubles for.

Firsthand Tips for Secondhand Cooks

According to Judy Kaminsky, the owner of Cookin', in San Francisco, there are several no-nos for cooking with secondhand pots and pans.

- Copper can be real trouble. Most copper pots are lined with another metal, such as nickel. If there is a break of any kind (check around the rivets and handles), don't cook with it. Cooking with raw copper can cause copper poisoning.
- Collect old ceramic crocks, but don't pickle in them. According to Kaminsky, old pickling residues trapped in the cracks might leach into the liquid.
- Cast-iron pans pose a problem for vegetarians. Beans and tomatoes tend to unseason the cast iron. Cook in an enameled cast-iron pan instead.
- A chip in an enamel pot inside or outside is not dangerous. If the chips are inside the pot or pan, a coating of cooking oil will help eliminate any metallic taste.
- To remove rust from, say, a cast-iron frying pan, scour with superfine steel wool and coat with a little cooking oil.

ellen O'Neill's summer kitchen, seen above, in Sag Harbor, New York, conjures up images of the farmhouse kitchen inhabited for years by TV's Walton family. Unlike the Walton kitchen, however, Ellen's has a heavy floral emphasis—rosebud wallpaper, dogwood dishes, a tulip quilt folded over the back of a park bench painted pink—the accent color, along with peach and green, of everything else in the kitchen. Ellen's style started to evolve in 1979, when she opened what she describes as a women's hardware store in New York City, filled with drawers and bins of old lace, ribbons, quilt patches, buttons, textiles, aprons, hats, and odd pieces of painted furniture. Ellen's fourteen-year-old daughter, Bridget, was just a baby then. "Of course I brought her. For her, it was like playing in a wonderful attic." After ten years of hard work and great success, she closed it down, and now forages not only for herself (for pleasure!) but to gather inspiration for an American designer who would be very much at home if he dropped by her cozy kitchen any morning.

Left: Ellen O'Neill loves the old-fashioned porcelain sink in her summer kitchen. "I'd never trade this in for a dishwasher. In the country I love the ritual." She loves letting the dishes dry in the open air in her Rubbermaid dish drainer. She loves washing them with her pink-and-white striped cotton dishrags, propped on the faucet. While she washes, Bridget or a guest can dry, resting on the little green metal chair that she picked up for $18 at the Southampton antiques show. The dishes themselves, arranged above on the pine shelves, rest against a backdrop of rosebud wallpaper. "They were my great-aunt Marion's, made by Franciscan Dinnerware in the forties." The extraneous pieces—bowls, pitchers, creamers, eggcups, salt and pepper shakers—were collected here and there from flea markets and shops, mostly in Sag Harbor. The pink-and-white juice glasses on the middle shelf at the far left were found at a favorite source, Kitschen, on Christopher Street in New York City—six for $15.

Above: The kitchen table (see the small picture on the opposite page) is actually an old barn door Ellen propped up on a pair of sawhorses and covered with kitcheny cotton fabric. The distressed white basket she paid $8 for has a broken bottom, but according to Ellen that's never been a problem—"because we never move it . . . it's a permanent fixture." Rather like a centerpiece, it is always showcasing something different—usually assorted old table linens, dish towels, place mats, and napkins, always in the pink family. The big conch, a seaworthy paperweight (or fabric weight), is known as "Bridget's Big Shell." The chipped handle on the ironstone pitcher—$15—behind it has not hindered its ability to pour milk or hold flowers.

Left: Bo, a guest's wire-haired fox terrier, awaits his mistress and her breakfast. The bench he has chosen to warm is collapsible—a portable park bench that Ellen bought at Brimfield Market in Brimfield, Massachusetts, for $40. She painted it pink, of course. She bought the appliquéd tulip quilt top, draped on the back of the bench, because its floral motif echoes the dogwood on Aunt Marion's china. The tea-bag holders next to the mugs and stacked on the shelf below were collected for about $1 each at various flea markets.

Above: Two of Ellen's old-fashioned favorites: crocheted potholders, picked up for an average of $3 each, and the dishrags from church sales—three for $1.

Left: Propped among Aunt Marion's Franciscan dinnerware is a pink volume entitled <u>Problems of Love and Marriage . . . Advice to the Love Lorn</u>, by Beatrice Fairfax. It was left by a friend once who let herself in unannounced, dropped it on the kitchen table, and left. "She got the color right, anyway," says Ellen with a laugh. Has she read it? She won't say.

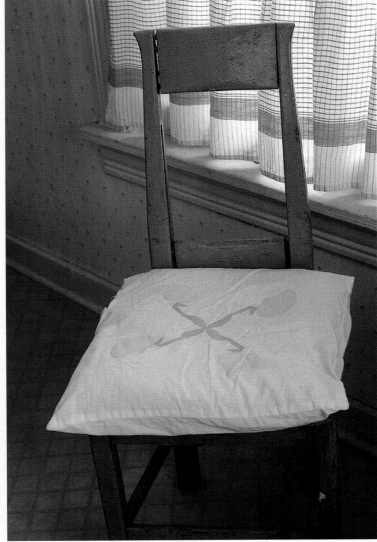

Above: Though she paid more for it than she wanted to—$50—the pink wood flowerpot stand had to come home with Ellen from the Brimfield Market. The $5 frame on top of it was a find from nearby Southampton. "It was the beading detail on the inside rim that drove me to it." It, too, needs some gluing!

Top right: In front of a kitchen window, curtained with dish-towel fabric, stands an old fragile student's chair in need of a little wood glue in the creases (see tips at right). The lower slat is adjustable to the sitter's back. The pillow is covered in a piece of quilt top appliquéd with tulips, similar to the one on the back of the bench on the opposite page.

Stay Glued: How to End the Wooden Wobblies

Many old wooden chairs have, after many years of bracing backs of all persuasions, developed a case of the wooden wobblies. Ellen recommends Elmer's Carpenter's Wood Glue. After an examination of the ailing piece, follow the directions on the back of the package. Spread the glue on both surfaces and clamp for 30 minutes, or, to be really sure, overnight. If you don't have a clamp or a vise handy, secure with a clothesline or bungee cord. If it's a smaller job, try cotton string, masking tape (keeping the sticky side away from the wood), elastic, or even thick rubber bands.

The only thing new in Ellen O'Neill's New York City dining room is the wallpaper. After it was put up in 1990, it looked too bright to her, so she had it whitewashed to fade the colors. (For other views and how to whitewash, see the next pages.) Chairs, dishes, table linens—all have that same whitewashed look, as if the sun had shone on them for many years, or as if they had all been swirled in milk. The small grooved bowl at right is the color of Chinese green-tea ice cream—"even softer!" says Ellen. "I love the way my fingers fit into those grooves," she adds. It cost $8 and was bought, along with the rest of the stack— the baby blue sandwich plate for $3 and the dusty pink soup bowls and dinner plates for $20—from Richard Camp, a dealer in Southampton. The teacups (part of a 26-piece set for $15) nested next to them are Lurayware from the forties, found in an antiques co-op in Ephrata, Pennsylvania, along Route 22, "where a stretch of antiques shops are open seven days a week," Ellen informs us. The little blue teapot didn't come with them. It's English, and came from the supplier of the other stack, Richard Camp, for $15. The odd couple of chairs pushed up to the table give the room a Swedish-cottage feeling. The keyhole chair on the right, one of a pair bought for $5 at a trash-and-treasure sale in Water Mill, New York, is paired with Ellen's Aunt Marion's sewing chair. "It's in desperate need of gluing," says Ellen. "The top comes off whenever it's moved."

Top right: The two damask tablecloths (in a wider view of the dining-room table seen on the previous pages), in need of a little pressing, were found in Ephrata, Pennsylvania. Layered over the white banquet cloth ($10) is a blue-and-white "topper," bought for $6. The single damask dinner napkin, bordered in pale green, is part of a set of four that cost $6. The second of the pair of key-shaped chairs is skirted with a blue-and-white checked seat cover, and topped with a foam cushion covered in a pale pink damask tea towel.

Middle, bottom, and far right: Yellowware mixing bowls and custard cups, glazed in unexpected colors, banded, and embossed, were produced by many potteries from the turn of the century well into the 1900s. Ellen's collection was gathered here and there at garage sales and at Brimfield, of course. It's mixed with miscellaneous piles of blue-and-white damask napkins and the green spindle-back chair, opposite page, found for $10—Ellen can't remember where.

How to Age New Wallpaper

Ellen used this technique to mellow a new, too-bright wallpaper. She also likes the "chalky" finish it left on the paper. You might consider it on old or new wallpaper that you've inherited. (I recently took down eight rooms of different wallpapers, preferring white walls, but if I had known about Ellen's whitewash fader, I might have experimented before taking everything down.) A professional painter, John Ralbovsky, did the job for Ellen. Before proceeding, he tested several pieces of the wallpaper with different strengths of whitewash formulas. If you don't have samples, test in an unobtrusive corner. (You can wipe it off if you don't like the result, but keep in mind the mixture dries very fast!) What you need is McKlosky's Glaze Coat, a transparent oil-based glaze, and Chromo Japan Paint (white), a highly pigmented paste color immersed in linseed oil that dries fast and flat—both can be found at most good paint stores, particularly those that cater to decorators. Experiment with different strengths, but as a rule of thumb Ralbovsky suggests ½ gallon of Glaze Coat to 3 teaspoons of Japan Paint. The color of your wallpaper will determine how strong the color of your mixture should be. Overestimate the degree of color necessary, anticipating the amount to be wiped off. Apply mix with a brush and then, using a soft rag or diaper, wipe it off with a circular motion to blur the brush strokes and give the surface a soft patina. Leave a little color on and try to keep the texture as smooth as possible.

How to Launder Old Linens

It might have been Ellen O'Neill's two great-aunts, who both ran dress shops in the forties, who started her on the road to loving old textiles. A cache of hers is seen at left. Below, her recipe for brightening up old linens.

"When you're dealing with old linens, you have to keep in mind that not all problems are solvable. You can never be sure how sturdy a cloth is or how fast its colors are. Follow my recipe only if you are willing to risk it all!

- "Most table linens of the dish-towel, napkin, and tablecloth variety can probably be thrown right into the washing machine with Clorox 2 and detergent on the gentle cycle. For those pieces that can't withstand the agitation of a washing machine, like fragile batiste, things with lace trim and insets, and very sheer fabrics, boiling them on top of the stove with bleach is a safer alternative.

- "Fill a big roasting pan with water and Snowy Bleach (to determine the exact amount, read the directions on the box) and bring to a boil on top of the stove.

- "Reduce heat to a simmer and submerge your linens with a long-handled wooden spoon. (I keep one just for that purpose, and a special pan, too.) Let simmer for ten minutes, stirring occasionally. The boiling separates the fibers. The bleach bubbles the dirt through. (This is a speedier process than the soaking-for-a-couple-of-days method.) Carefully empty into a deep sink or tub, and run under lukewarm water (cold water shrinks the fabric). Towel dry and fold into white plastic garbage bags and refrigerate for at least an hour or up to a week. Iron them right out of the refrigerator. They're slightly stiff, so no starch is necessary. Heavier items may require steam or spraying with water. They'll smell wonderfully hygienic."

- For really tough stains, Ellen has discovered Z'Out, a concentrated stain remover. The Vermont Country Store carries this through their catalog. Their phone number is (802) 362-2400 (no collect calls, please). Their address: The Vermont Country Store, Mail Order Office, P.O. Box 3000, Manchester Center, VT 05255-3000.

animal house

Bix and Ruby, two black standard poodles, live with their adoptive mother, Judyth vanAmringe, in a wonderful loftlike duplex in New York City. For a while, she owned another pair—the two cast-cement poodles ("fifties garden ornamentalia") seen on the opposite page, bottom row. Does she have a large collection of other poodle stuff? "Oh, no," she exclaims. "I have the <u>real</u> thing, I don't need replicas." Lora Zarubin, a New York City restaurateur (see pages 206–207) and wire-haired fox terrier owner, is much more representative of animal and dog memorabilia collectors. The scruffy pack of her favorite breed in stuffed animal form is seen at left, top and bottom, in her New York City bedroom. What led to Robert Miles Runyon's life-sized replica of a cow turned into a bar in his Manhattan Beach, California, living room is another matter entirely. See for yourself on page 116, and on the way look out for mice (one's rather famous), white rabbits, a pair of goats, a squirrel, wild turkeys, a horse, and a little fuzzy creature with a white stripe down his back.

Opposite, clockwise from top left: An oil painting of an English springer spaniel at Ruby Beets in Bridgehampton, New York, which cost $25; a pencil drawing of a beagle found in Virginia for $15; under a mural of a dog of undetermined breed, given to Lora Zarubin by the artist, is a lineup of her wire-haired fox terriers; looking as if it's just seen a mouse, Lora's dogpack has taken refuge in a child's Adirondack rocker; a produce basket painted, collaged, and mounted on a twig stand ($2 at a barn sale) gets a doggy bone for most imaginative whatchamacallit; Judyth vanAmringe's guard-dog poodles; an old varsity sweater with a sewed-on bulldog mascot, which cost $8 at Pontes Antiques in Kill Devil Hills, North Carolina; and a pincushion retriever with a nose for measuring (a tape's inside it!), found at the Twenty-sixth Street flea market in New York City for $5.

Previous pages: A Saint Bernard for sale at New York's Twenty-sixth Street flea market for $85.

Right: The designer Ron Meyer's studio in Los Angeles (which once was a garage— see page 46) resembles the den of an extravagant and slightly sloppy pirate who has let his plunder of fringes, rich-textured tapestries, gilt mirrors, bolts of satin, and coils of silken cords drip luxuriously all over the place. It is a most intriguing hodgepodge of bits and pieces collected for various clients and projects—some destined never to leave the studio. One that might fall into this category is the shaggy guard at the entrance—a hand-painted old English sheepdog. (How capable he is of fulfilling his duty is debatable, owing to the mop of hair that must in some way impede his vision and a broken right front paw that detaches itself whenever he is moved around.) Ron purchased him at Butterfield's Auction House in San Francisco about eight years ago for less than $50. The vase-shaped splat-back chair that is the temporary guardhouse is English as well. Ron found it at the Pasadena City College flea market for $30 or $40 "with a thought to having its comfortable proportions copied." The frayed seat attests to its constant use. The very blond and carefully coiffed lady in profile, painted in the fifties, was purchased for $100 from Abell's Auction Company in Commerce, a suburb of Los Angeles, several years ago. "It's not a brilliant painting," Ron confesses, "but I loved her style and had in mind to give her to a friend who loves that era. She is part of my friend's world now."

Above: At last count Alice and Don Reid, antiques dealers in Livingston, New York, had six dogs—three Newfoundlands (Geronimo, Stormy, and Tigger), two black Labradors (Arrow and Zephyr), and a yellow Labrador named Yeltsin. All and all that adds up to about 675 pounds of furry, licking, romping animals. It's no surprise, then, that scattered throughout their late-nineteenth-century farmhouse (for more see pages 116–117 and 149) there are little altars to dogs and dogdom. One of the most prominent is on top of an old Shaker cupboard in their living room. Front and center sits a black-and-white plaster spaniel, the kind popular in the thirties and forties as carnival prizes (see page 132 for more on carnival prizes) but also sold in dime stores as cheap decorative pieces. "He was probably one of the latter," suggests Alice, "sold at a Grant's or Woolworth's for what I got him for at a yard sale—a dollar!" He was manufactured by the St. Louis Missouri Art Company; his identification is marked on the bottom—Robia Ware, #373. The book standing on end, <u>Storm, Dog of Newfoundland</u>, by Anthony Von Eisen, published in 1948, was a Father's Day present to Don from daughter Cindy, for $20. The wooden cat toy (planning an escape up the side of Alice's old field basket) is new. Alice paid $6 for it at an import store. When the handles are squeezed, the cat, which has articulated limbs, flips over the rod his front paws are attached to. The two Mexican religious statues, known as <u>santos</u>, were bought with another one for $160 at an auction. The rest—the clay sombrero and three pieces of glazed pottery—are Mexican "souvenir stuff" bought together at an estate sale for $2. Showcasing them all is a primitive version of what looks like the Hollywood Bowl—an old sleigh "headboard." At its pinnacle is an iron eagle head with rattan wings forming two shields, designed to protect sleigh riders from flying snow and mud.

Looking a little like David, a small wooden black-cat pepper shaker stands up to a towering Goliath—a skimpily clad mouse doll—amid other small items for sale at Stuckey's Antique Emporium in Richmond, Virginia. Peppy, identified by the hand-painted name on the shaker (see it on the following pages), offers a triple threat to pepper lovers. When Peppy is shaken, not only does pepper, stored in the barrel beneath, flow out of his screw-top head but his green irises wobble frantically and a distinct "meow" arises from a "voice box" hidden in his base. He probably was made in the forties, when figural and souvenir salt and pepper shakers were in high demand. Missing his partner (Salty?), Peppy is a little less collectible, but combining as he does the functions of toy and table accessory he seems rather a rare cat on his own —especially for the $2 ($1 off the marked price!) I paid. His giant friend or adversary (whatever the case may be) is without question one of the many Disney characters licensed in the wake of <u>Steamboat Willie</u>, Mickey's first movie, made in 1928. Though her anatomy makes it questionable whether she is Mickey or Minnie, the red hair ribbon is the obvious clincher. A rubber squeeze doll from the fifties or early sixties, she was marked at $30. Disneyana, as it is known by collectors, is a category beginners may want to avoid. Though the most collectible, and expensive, items are from the thirties, almost any item from any year tends to be priced on the high side.

Above: Peppy the cat—a wooden pepper shaker seen on the previous pages—joined a menagerie on top of a bookshelf in our living room at Elm Glen Farm. His resting place, beneath a long-necked goose handcarved by a driftwood sculptor from the Outer Banks of North Carolina, is a little handmade wooden sewing box with hand-painted replicas of what it holds inside—a tape measure and spools of thread. I picked it up in a country store in East Hampton, New York, for about $20. The tartan box with wooden handles to the left is a biscuit tin from the 1940s, found at the Watnot Shop in Hudson, New York. The primitive waterfall painting with the three-dimensional stag was also found there, for $15. The pinecone drawing to the left, simply signed "Fred," was $2 at another shop in the area. The plaster bas-relief of the elk at the far right, a wall plaque (too heavy to hang), was a Christmas present more than six years ago from my mother. With the exception of Peppy and the sewing box, I collected all these objects for display in a former, more primitive house with white plaster walls. When we bought this house, the toile de Jouy wallpaper was a bit of a jolt, but somehow it all worked together until last winter, when I stripped it off. The white plaster walls are back, but some days I miss those little blue-and-white scenes of family, sheep, and old-fashioned waterwheels. The collections of D. H. Lawrence, Isak Dinesen, and Gene Stratton Porter seen below were found at Howard Frisch's Antiquarian Books, in Livingston, New York, run by Howard Frisch and Fred Harris.

Left: Think of this bookshelf as Alice Reid does, not only as a storage place for books but as a high-rise for all kinds of animal tenants. In the penthouse (the top shelf, of course) resides a dappled papier-mâché pony—a Victorian pull toy on a little wheeled wooden platform. Alice secured him, her first tenant, at a yard sale nearby. "I loved his ratty little horsehair tail," she remarks. Three stories down, sharing space with books entitled <u>American Historical Spoons</u> and <u>The Ornamented Tray</u>, live a pair of plaster sheep, bookends from the twenties. "Four dollars for the two," says Alice, "because one had a slightly damaged ear." The floor below is shared by <u>Four Little Bunnies</u>, a book from the twenties, which contains photographs of live rabbits dressed up and posed as humans (a precursor to William Wegman's dog portraits?). Alice bought it only after she was reassured by a note from the author that none of the animals suffered anything during the process (except a little humiliation, perhaps). Next to them is a stack of Billy Whiskers books, celebrating the great adventures of a well-loved and -traveled goat, published in the early 1900s and written by Frances Trego Montgomery, with great illustrations by F. J. Murch. "I got a batch of ten or twelve at Brimfield Market in Massachusetts seven years ago for thirty dollars." The last tenant, poking his head out of an alleyway of books at the far right, is a shy little homemade lamb's-wool dog, found hidden in a $2 box lot of old football gear at an auction in Rhinebeck, New York.

Above: "The Cow Bar," as it is referred to, was installed in the
Manhattan Beach, California, home of the graphic artist Robert
Miles Runyon in 1983, after a lot of creative "angsting" to come
up with something totally unbelievable. "I think we did it," suggests the owner. The cow itself (the kind you see in front of a
Dairy Queen) was bought from a shop that custom-makes specialty
items like this for retailers and film studios. "It was totally over-
hauled," reports Runyon, "with new teeth, new eyes, and a refrigerator inside. This cow dispenses chilled champagne instead of
milk," he says with a laugh. Guests who pull up a chair to the
glass ledge that surrounds it receive a little enamel cow pin as a
souvenir of their visit. Stretched on the wall behind the cow (you
can just glimpse the bottom) is a rare 18′ × 9′ American circus
poster from the 1920s that Runyon bought from a friend who
found a stash of them in a barn in Kansas. "It was probably the
site of the circus's last performance before it went broke."

Left: Though dogs (as you have read previously on page 111) are her abiding passion (really big dogs—Newfoundlands and Labradors, currently), Alice Reid has found room in her heart and on her kitchen shelves to honor other (really big) animals as well. Her cow creamer, on the bottom shelf, is "an Elsie Borden kind of cow," suggests Alice, from the twenties or thirties, found in a dime store for 10 cents or a quarter. It was a gift from her mother-in-law. The heavy metal steer above it, another gift from Alice's mother-in-law, is of the Highland breed (mostly raised in Scotland, the homeland of her mother-in-law) and was probably part of a child's farm set from the forties. Around the corner, sitting comfortably on the edge, is a dog known for its courage—a Saint Bernard, complete with keg made of sterling silver ("a hundred-dollar splurge at an auction"). The three dog mugs, one per shelf, were originally part of a cider set—very popular in the late 1800s. Hers were a present from a dog-loving friend, and similar sets are now easy flea-market pickups for a dollar or two. Hanging in the window is a colorful string of pinecones, pods, and gourds, a common decorative souvenir of the Southwest in the 1930s and 1940s that was based on the popular legend of Ramona and Allesandro. These star-crossed lovers would leave each other tokens such as these as a form of secret communication— a pinecone might mean "Meet me under the pine tree tonight." Supposedly, Ramona saved all these things and strung them together. The pair Alice bought at a yard sale for $1 were hand made by Max Roisman (so the tag that came with them states), of 1308 West 130th Street, Gardena, California. Further, it reads, "Good Luck Comes to Him Who Buys a Charm String on a Whim."

"Meow, meow . . ." Indeed, that could be the sound of the real live cats belonging to Grace Coddington (see pages 44 and 168–171), but, then again, it could be sound coming from Grace's kitchen, the residence of the five felines seen in this picture. A beckoning cat, such as the two seen in the form of ceramic teapots below, is a symbol of welcome in Japan. Grace bought the little yellow one on a trip to China. The orange tabby was made by the English potters Wood and Son, and is marked "Pussyfoot" on the bottom. It and the two to the left were collected at the Chelsea Antiques Market in London in the early 1970s. How much? "Not much," says Grace. My guess—a pound or two or maybe five. The little black cat without a spout is undoubtedly English—made to hold sugar? The littlest of the litter, a cocoa-colored chap standing on his hind legs (to appear taller?), would serve barely a cup.

In the corner of a shelf shared with a family of four wooden balusters (one sporting a nest toupee) salvaged from old houses in Vermont and Long Island is Sharone Einhorn's own little museum of natural history—a white rabbit preserved in a glass habitat box that she rescued years ago from a dusty Long Island antiques shop for $20. The bench below, $150, camouflaging an old steam radiator, once sat on the porch of The Shady Lake Lodge in the Catskill Mountains of New York. Its faded colors were the inspiration for Sharone's "whirlpool green" paint job on the walls. "I mixed the green latex with a glaze —a real no-no because it separates like oil and water—but I loved the distressed-looking result, which I intensified by scratching it with sharp sticks and scrapers." The photograph of Native Americans dated 1888—Mohawks, Sharone thinks—was found in upstate New York for $75. The chandelier, romantically draped with cheesecloth, was "very cheap." Its single light bulb, she confesses, "is not very flattering to dinner guests sitting beneath it." More flattering is the light from the single candle held by a Russian silver candleholder, one of a pair that belonged to Sharone's grandparents. The frosted etched-glass vase—"not Lalique" but probably an inexpensive American copy—was inspired by the French master's Art Deco pieces of the early 1930s.

121

On the far left corner of my desk (for a fuller view see page 34), a papier-mâché squirrel from down Mexico way, bought at a folk art shop in New York for $10, looks dazed as he spies at the opposite end a cast-iron furry friend (or foe?), intent, judging by his pose, on wreaking vengeance. The skunk's tail is wire, covered with some kind of furry material—unidentifiable since its foray into the jaws of a curious (real) puppy. I bought him for $12 in 1988 on a trip to Houston, Texas, at a shop called Room Service. The alarm clock, a present, no longer tick-tocks, but I love its fat numbers and its old green paint. The little yellow typewriter-ribbon can with a silhouette of a southern belle on top bore a message (printed on the top) from my friend Alice Reid: "Carter's Valiant." It was made by the Carter's ink company in the 1940s.

f this be the Mad Hatter's tea party, then that must be the white rabbit himself (far right), striking a very unrabbit-like pose on a fine mahogany chair. He seems a tad impatient, as does his only other guest, the long-haired cat at the far left (though not the Cheshire). With five cups set, it would seem that three guests are still in question. The oak Welsh cupboard behind them is filled with (shhhh) their mother's (Liza Carter Norton's) eclectic mix of pottery, fine porcelain, and majolica teapots, pitchers, bowls, and plates, picked up in flea markets in New York City, in London, and in Paris for from $6 to $20.

Costume Collecting

Halloween costumes such as these, which have been around since the 1920s, are increasingly popular collectibles, according to Sam Cornish, president of Collegeville Costume Company in Collegeville, Pennsylvania. Collegeville manufactured their first in 1926, and went on to introduce a slew of celebrity characters (Howdy Doody for one) that included many animals—Bugs Bunny and the Looney Tunes gang were very big in the forties and fifties. "Collectors should start in their attics, then scour flea markets, particularly those in Pennsylvania," suggests Jerry Harmyck of U.S.E.D., a shop in New York City. "Pennsylvanians take their Halloween seriously because so many of its German immigrants celebrated <u>Fasching</u>" (a pre-Lenten dress-up-in-costumes-kind-of tradition, not unlike Mardi Gras in New Orleans). Jerry says good vintage costumes can be picked up for $25 to $100. So save those Ninja Turtles costumes!

child's play

In 1976, on a business trip to a small town outside Cleveland, Ohio, I wandered into a little junk shop and found my dollhouse, missing since I was ten. Well, of course, it wasn't the very dollhouse I owned but one exactly like it. (Mine had been lost in a fire.) I paid $10 and carried it out like Lancelot clasping the Holy Grail (see it on page 140). Everyone's got a story like that—toys from our childhood can zap a memory back like nothing else can. Otherwise, why would we cling to our old falling-apart teddy bears or the silly little playthings of childhood? Some people (call them childish, perhaps) have made up their minds that old games, lucky charms, dolls, playhouses, carnival prizes, tea sets, and Mickey Mouse are okay to have around all the time for visual entertainment, inspiration, fantasy, and humor. Their credo: Age doesn't matter when you're having fun!

Previous pages: A little girl named Dot who grew up in the twenties hoarded each little plastic charm that came her way, whether tucked in a candy box or packaged with a stick of gum. Twenty years ago, she packed them off to her nephew Doug Taylor, who has collected things like this since he was a child (see pages 24–27 and 72–73) and who found the perfect porcelain box to keep them in. "It reminded me of a piece from a witch's vanity set, with all those funny points." Over the years he has added more charms (their actual size—one half inch).

Opposite, bottom left: Doug Taylor's collection of games, puzzles, and children's activity sets was assembled over the course of more than twenty years, mostly for about 25 cents each. One of his favorites, made by McLoughlin Brothers of New York—one of the most important game makers in America—was called Laughing Larry. Worth at least $1,000 today, the box and its pieces were bought for $2 in 1970.

Opposite, top left: "Most of these toys I got in the seventies at Chicago's drive-in movie trunk-show markets," reports Doug Taylor. "People just drove their cars in and opened the trunks." Besides Felix the Cat (dead center), one of Doug's favorites is the chicken with the top hat on (above Felix), a hollow papier-mâché character meant to be filled with Easter candy.

Opposite, bottom right: Aunt Dot's doll, another gift to Doug, resembles Scootles, a doll manufactured by Cameo Doll Products Company in 1930. If found today, dressed in her original clothes, she'd be worth around $400. The clothes were hand made by Doug's great-aunt Lilly.

Opposite, top right: Doug found this box of cutout paper dolls from the early 1940s at a flea market for 10 cents. Starting in the late 1800s, paper dolls were given away as a cheap form of advertising. Companies like Kellogg's tucked them into their cereal boxes in the 1920s. By the forties, every movie star worthy of the name was the model for a paper-doll collection. Rock Hudson, Elizabeth Taylor, Betty Grable, and Shirley Temple spawned hundreds. Uncut books, sheets, or boxed sets are much more valuable than those already cut.

Above: A red beanie encrusted with plastic Cracker Jack charms from the early fifties (a clue to its date of origin is a miniature license plate dated 1951) was a birthday present to my husband, Howard, in 1985. I found it at a flea market in upstate New York, and upon discovering not only some of his favorite hobbies and foods represented, but (lo and behold!) his very own initials—"HB"—embossed in gold paint on two separate black plastic squares, I knew this was a purchase meant to be. I happily paid the $30.

Left: In Miriam Wosk's home office in Los Angeles, the gleaming white work surfaces are interrupted here and there with the colorful, whimsical souvenirs of years of ardent flea-market foraging. Lying about in profusion are what appear to be the toys of Miriam's five-year-old son, Adam. "He would certainly enjoy them," she admits, "but they came into being way before he was even a consideration." She adds, "I like to bring art into everyday life." Her desk, seen in detail above, speaks well of that sentiment.

Opposite, top: Miriam's artful clutter inspires her daily. She particularly enjoys the quartet of friendly faces looking on as she works (from left to right): a smiling clown, a painted wooden artifact from an old thirties arcade game; a ceramic head of a lady, part of Miriam's large collection of sculptural vases (see another on pages 58—59), called into service here to hold a bouquet of rulers; Charlie McCarthy, another wooden cutout, with hooks on the bottom (meant to hold keys or pot holders?); and a freckle-face mug, which Miriam interprets as "a little girl" and I challenge with "monkey face"! The red plastic Schaefer beer display unit filled with pens and pencils is a perfect example of Wosk efficiency and aesthetics in action. "In a different context, cheap advertising gimmicks take on a new kind of usefulness as well as artfulness," she suggests. Below it rests another clown—a baby-food dish from the 1940s, a little green due to (possibly) a compartmentalized stomach full of push pins and colorful paper clips. Almost everything here was collected from the Rose Bowl flea market in Pasadena for no more than $25.

Left: More than a decade ago, when Miriam Wosk bought this chair and two others at a floor-sample sale in a New York City department store, they were upholstered in brown calico fabric. When they arrived home, she couldn't stand the fabric, and almost immediately took out her brushes and acrylic paints and, using the old fabric as a canvas, created one of her early works featuring Mickey Mouse.

"How much is that doggy, piggy, elephant, horsey, birdie in the window?" was a question directed over and over again to Judyth vanAmringe, the owner of this grand menagerie of more than 400 vintage (twenties to late fifties) chalkware carnival prizes, which made an unprecedented appearance in the 12′ × 12′ window of her shop in New York City in the fall of 1991. Mass-produced by novelty companies and enterprising individuals in their garages, the figures' individuality came mostly from the choice of spray-paint colors and sparkly glitter used to finish them off. You can find them as she did at flea markets, yard sales, and junk shops for as little as $15 or as much as $250.

Left: On the work counter of my summer atelier at Elm Glen Farm (see page 151) stand two chalkware figurines from my minuscule (as compared to that seen on the preceding pages) collection. The larger one, 20″ tall, of a young ringleted girl and her begging dog, I bought for $12 from a woman nearby who opens her two barns, filled with tag-sale collectibles, to the public on most summer weekends. It was probably sold as an inexpensive decorative item (for a child's room, no doubt) at a Grant's or Woolworth's in the forties. Then, it might have cost a dollar or two. Her little sailor friend, half her size, is none other than Shirley Temple. Because her image was mass-produced without permission (as were the likenesses of many other celebrities), she was referred to simply as the Smile Doll. To her right is a portrait of a pigtailed girl I picked up recently at a church flea market for $1. In between the two is a dog cutout made with a bandsaw, found in a San Francisco thrift shop, Krims Krams, for $3. The big flowered vase at left, badly chipped, came from a yard sale for $5. The berried branches are summer honeysuckle.

If most people saw what Judyth vanAmringe sees each morning when she opens her eyes—the little shingled playhouse pictured above and at left—they'd probably roll over and think they were still dreaming. "That's why I put it just <u>there</u>," she says, beaming. This wondrous plaything, so unexpected anywhere, but especially in a New York City apartment, was discovered leaning against a bright old orange Mercedes at an upstate New York flea market in 1987. Judyth paid about $1,000 for it, and though she is quite confident it was always just a facade, she has no idea what it was originally intended for. "More than likely it was a stage set of some kind," she surmises. It's about six feet tall and came with the surrounding picket fence and gate. A friend added the flower boxes under the two shuttered windows, and Judyth stuck in seed packets that had pictures of giant blooming pansies. The watering can is a child's toy from the forties. Judyth made the bouquet on the front door out of big buttons covered with jolly printed fabrics.

If Judyth vanAmringe's playhouse, seen on the previous pages, had three more walls and a furnished interior, I'd imagine a mantelpiece in it like the one seen here, salvaged from an old house in upstate New York by a dealer who charged me $50 for it. I then brought it to our farmhouse and decorated it with tag-sale treasures I collected over a period of six months from New York to San Francisco. At either end stand one-of-a-kind (I'm sure of that!) glass oil lamps encrusted with costume jewelry glued on in highly sophisticated mosaic patterns. The owner of the Motherway Boutique, a thrift shop "of the unusual" on Fillmore Street in San Francisco, reluctantly sold them to me for $80. (Yes, they really work.) The pair of figurines next to them—Staffordshire knockoffs that cost $1—have the most grotesque facial expressions, due to a failed attempt at repainting them. The pair of illustrated tin children's plates, bought for $4, behind the woman are from Ohio, a shop in Venice, California (see page 96). The sugar bowl doubling as a bud vase was a "made-in-Japan" cheapie picked up for 25 cents. The two upright tin party horns on either side of the Native American chalkware statue—which was found at The Flying Duck in Stuyvesant, New York, for $12— were $1 apiece at a tag sale off Route 22 near Millerton, New York. The miniature souvenir mug filled with Queen Anne's lace was 50 cents. Behind it is what looked to me like a Matisse drawing on gold-painted wood—$2 at a tag sale. The paint-by-number seascape above it, in a plastic sparkle frame, was pulled out of a "10¢ each" box at a roadside tag sale along with the one on the other side of the mirror. The gilt-framed mirror cost $8 and was foraged from a flea market during my gold period (see pages 54–57).

Above: This painted table and two chairs were found at a store in East Hampton, New York, for $50. I love the look of them, and they're a good size for my carnival figurines, ready to dive into doll-sized wedges of watermelon. The plastic cacti were found at a flea market for a quarter.

Right: After the retrieval of my childhood dollhouse in 1976, I put it away, and then three years later began madly to decorate it. My two sons, Carter and Sam (six and three at the time), agreed, reluctantly at first, to lend me a hand, and as time went by got totally into it. Toward the end of the project (a summer), Carter and Sam picked out a little Georgia O'Keeffe-looking doll in a long prairie dress to live in the house and run things. (I never understood their name for her—"Fun Girl!") Though I insisted on all the furniture being wood, the whole job was probably done for less than $100. Some of the pieces were old, but most were brand new, handmade by a wonderful craftsman who lived near the house we stayed in that summer near Flemington, New Jersey.

Above: The first time I went to Such-a-Deal, a shop outside San Francisco, in Oakland, specializing in (so the card reads) "Junque, funk, and furniture," it was closed. I was frantic because I was leaving the next day, the shop hadn't been easy to get to, and, most of all, there in the window was a child's shopping cart that I couldn't live without. When I got back to my hotel I left a rather anxious message on an answering machine and set up an appointment with the owners to go back that night. The shopping cart (which I got) was not a "deal" at $95, but I felt it was unique, graphically representing the grocery-store products of the fifties and sixties. It features such well-known brands as Swift's Premium ham, Kleenex tissues, Borden's chocolate milk, Jell-O gelatin, Del Monte catsup, Kraft caramels, and even Skippy peanut butter (see next pages for a closer look). The cart made it safely back to New York in our plane's overhead luggage compartment.

Left: The little cart in our kitchen in upstate New York was pushed in by my five-year-old niece Cary Hunter, to help unload real bags of groceries.

The outside and inside panels of this child's shopping cart from the fifties (see previous pages) were probably produced in much the same way as the vivid old board games of the middle nineteenth to early twentieth centuries—lithographed artwork glued onto sturdy cardboard. To clean games, shopping carts, or any collectible of this sort, don't hesitate to use a little mild soap and warm water. Just wipe with a damp sponge or cloth so as not to disturb old glue.

junk masters

Junk masters are artists who for one reason or another will never be given a museum retrospective, will not be indexed in the annals of art history, will not be compared to Matisse or Picasso, and will never be an answer in the New York Times crossword puzzle. Art students, grandmothers, children, prison inmates, retired businessmen—they each had a vision that somewhere along the line got shoved in a box, and, like the portrait at left, ended up in a junk shop. A happier ending is given on page 157, one of many happy endings in this chapter, which is dedicated to those unsung junk masters waiting to be discovered just around the corner at the next tag sale, thrift shop, antiques store, or flea market.

Above: Unaccustomed to toile de Jouy and organza curtains, the mighty stag portrayed in oils, bought for $20 in a country store on Long Island, is somewhat encouraged by the rolling hills outside his new home in upstate New York. I propped him against the wall years ago, meaning to frame him properly. Chances are I never will. The farm scene above him cost three times as much at the Rhinebeck, New York, Antiques Show.

Left: For more on this mysterious man abandoned in a cardboard box and sold to me for $5 at Stuckey's Antique Emporium in Richmond, Virginia, see page 157.

Previous pages: A gallery of junk masters for sale at Bottle Shop Antiques in Washington Hollow, New York. The little shack over the water reminded me of a favorite summer cottage rented years ago in Old Nag's Head, North Carolina. For $15, it's mine forever.

Left: In a cozy corner of Alice and Don Reid's Columbia County, New York, living room hangs a not-so-permanent exhibition. To the left of a Native American weaving, bought at a Quaker meetinghouse sale for $3, are two oils. The upper one, a portrait of a man in a cotton field, has been attributed to a student of the New Orleans painter William Aiken Walker and was sold for $125. The one below, a Gurkha, Alice suggests, was $30. The illustration of the Native American framed below the blanket, bought for $12, dates from 1780.

Below left: Over a growing pile of bedside reading floats a tilting ex-voto—a religious tableau painted on tin. I picked it up for $15 in a shop in Sag Harbor, New York, more than ten years ago. The cutout paper hand silhouetted on black—a gift—resembles the mannequin's hand on the opposite page. Below it is <u>Brenda Knitting</u>, an oil I bought in a London flea market for $25. According to the framer's note on the back, Brenda is Scottish. To me she looks remarkably like the very English author of <u>To the Lighthouse</u>.

Far left, clockwise from top: A trio of family portraits was found at the Bermondsey flea market in London for a few pounds. Below them, the portrait of a man in a blue shirt (seen in its eventual home, page 151) was found for $5 in this rather surreal flea-market setting. The landscape below (seen on page 153) was $1. To the left of it, the bearded man, brother of the sisters above, is seen again on page 150.

It was a black-and-white photograph of Monet in his Paris studio, dwarfed by a forty-foot ceiling and walls filled top to bottom with his own masterpieces, that inspired my summer atelier housed in the top of our carriage house, seen above. Built more than one hundred fifty years ago in upstate New York, it had been the carpentry workshop of one of the former owners, who had added electricity and two full-length counters to sustain his handiwork far into the night. I had one counter dismantled to make room for an iron bed, an old kitchen table, a Louis XV chair, a church pew, a screened-in cupboard, a hat rack, and numerous chairs—all bought in one night at one auction. The other counter, seen at right under the windows, was left in place to service lots of simultaneous artistic expression. Several coats of white paint were spread over the rough wide boards of the interior to showcase my junk masters collection.

Above: A long view of the hayloft atelier. The counter was once a workbench.

Far left: Daylight floods the studio from two tall, skinny windows, seen from the exterior in the small picture at the far left. Artwork displayed inside includes a shack on the water, seen close up on pages 144–145, found framed for $15 at Bottle Shop Antiques in Dutchess County, New York. The pair of golden Oriental portraits in tin relief were brought back from a thrift shop in San Francisco for $10. The rather stern portrait above was from a batch picked up in the Bermondsey flea market in London for $5 apiece. Underneath the counter, slightly obscured, is an original watercolor by a good friend, Marcia Mossack.

Left: Displayed over the bed is a trio of oil paintings. The two at left, both tropically themed and both painted on canvas, were found in upstate New York. On the back of the one on top is scrawled in ballpoint pen: "Artist—J.E. Cook, my 3rd painting, 2/15/62, oil painted this Hawaiian seen [sic] on top of another one." Inscribed on the back of the one below, depicting nesting flamingos, is "painted during my leisure moments especially for Mary. Fondly, Ernest." There is no date. (Could the surname of this Ernest and his Mary by any chance be Hemingway? And the setting of his gift be none other than their home in Key West? Let's pretend—yes!) It's marked $3.50 but was a gift. To their right, found at The Joneses of Great Barrington, Massachusetts, is a portrait of a blue-shirted man who strongly resembles the artist Diego Rivera. He cost $5. The mustard-colored velvet chair, a Louis XV, was picked up at a local auction for $15.

finding frames for junk masters' works is not difficult. Consider, for example, the stack at right, piled up at a junk shop in Massachusetts. The blue one was found not five feet from the unframed oil of a fantastic tiger, seen in full on the following pages, that it seemed created for. If you're on a search for frames, it's helpful to keep a list of approximate dimensions in your wallet. (You never know when you'll come upon the right candidates.) Sometimes, found works of art look best unframed. I've been known many a time to unframe what I've bought or to bicker with the owner for a better price on the work without the frame. Often a dealer will put something in what she thinks is a glorious gilt frame and then jack up the price. If it's the painting you're interested in, see if the owner will sell it without the frame—for a better price, of course! Hang up your unframed works just to get used to them. Don't delay the joy of viewing them immediately. Eventually, you may find a frame you love, construct one yourself, or decide the painting is glorious on its own.

Above: Plaster fruits arranged in a Mexican enamel dish, all from Such-a-Deal in Oakland, California, and all costing $4, suggest a still-life subject worthy of the brush of Bonnard.

Left: Two disparate pieces of pottery set before a backdrop of framed and unframed paintings conjure up images of Impressionist colors. The smaller, marbleized piece, $1, displays a collection of calligraphy pens picked up at flea markets for an average of 50 cents. The larger vase, offering no clues to its origin, was bought because it brought to mind the still lifes of Matisse. The landscapes behind it, stacked precariously one on top of the other, were each $1. The books spread out on the table are French schoolbooks about <u>les animaux</u> brought back from a Paris flea market. For a larger view, turn the page.

The wall that Monet's Giverny studio inspired rises thirty feet at its highest point. The challenge of filling it like his was begun with the tiger painting found for $5 unframed at The Joneses in Great Barrington, Massachusetts. The portrait of a lady (could it be Tallulah Bankhead?) above it and the still life to the left were both found in a pile of dusty canvases at The Bottle Shop in Washington Hollow, New York, for $10 and $15, respectively. The small still life of tulips was done by my sister on a weekend visit. The two to the right, both by the same artist, were bought at New York City's Twenty-sixth Street flea market for $75 and $50 (inflated city prices!). The map of Ontario over the bed cost $5 at an upstate New York flea market. Scattered on the table are old prints found at a church tag sale for 25 cents each.

Right: It's not surprising that Ron Meyer, a painter and designer of romantic interiors (he just finished his second nightclub in Los Angeles), fell madly in love with this very romantic portrait of a lady, done in oil on paper. He first laid eyes on her at the Long Beach flea market three years ago. In his estimation, he paid "nothing for her." She was $15, framed. A painter of portraits himself (see page 46), Ron is particularly partial to those of the nineteenth century. His guess is that this lady was done around 1840. "I love the strictness of her dress and then the surprise of the little corsage over her heart. She's a real nineteenth-century American woman." Propped on a chair draped with a machine-made piece of tapestry probably from the same period, which was bought at auction for a client's chair—"He never got it!"—she looks more than revered.

Below: Ron Meyer shudders to think how he almost missed this study of faces painted on canvas, which he found at a flea market for $1. It was on the back of a very bad art-school portrait that he just happened to turn over. Tacked on the wall of his design studio, gasping for air behind bolts and remnants of fabric, it remains one of his favorite finds.

Left: There is an Unknown Soldier kind of quality about portraits found unsigned and unidentified—like this man in an open-collared white shirt hanging on another wall of my summer atelier (seen on pages 150–155). Who was he? His image was found in a cardboard box (see page 146) on the second floor of a junk shop in Richmond, Virginia. The cost was $5. He has the look of an educated man, perhaps a writer. His hairline would indicate an age of around forty-something. The style suggests the 1930s. Perhaps he's not a writer. He could be an artist, and this is his self-portrait. He seems a bit tortured. He lives near the water, has a beautiful old sailboat that belonged to his father and will one day belong to his son, who is living with his mother. The nice thing about paintings without histories is that you can invent them yourself. What's not invented is the chair next to him, a weathered Adirondack similar in texture to the painting. It went for $35 at an auction in Dutchess County, New York. The felt flower pillow, $1 at a tag sale, adds a romantic touch, like the corsage on the lady on the opposite page.

157

Spring's eternal in Ellen O'Neill's sunny apartment in upper Manhattan. (For more on Ellen, see pages 98–105.) The blue-and-white striped wallpaper helps. So does the crisp white dresser cloth spread on top of the old painted cupboard filled with quilts, tablecloths, curtain remnants, slipcover pieces, and Beacon blankets. But mostly it's the signs of spring in the two paintings propped on top that give the room its cool serenity. The lady on the right arrived six years ago—"lent by a friend for something I can't recall," Ellen laments. "Let's say she came to visit and never left. The truth is I can't let her go. She has such stature, and of course I love the faded colors, the dress, and the knot of hair. She's pretty old, probably nineteenth century." The pastoral scene to her left was found in a flea market in Brimfield, Massachusetts. It was one of a pair bought for $15. "I loved the barn, the colors, and even the hole!" The blue-and-white plaid biscuit tin with oak handles, bought for $10, is a repository for "drawer-fill." Ellen used to sell the wooden robin's eggs in her store for 75 cents— "They're speckled, very big at Easter," she adds. The shawl, folded on top of the cigar box above them, is woolen challis, complete with moth holes. The pamphlet is entitled Steps to Achievement.

"**e**veryman a Rembrandt!" has been the Craft Master promise since the late forties, when Max Klein of the Palmer Paint Company of Detroit, Michigan, teamed up with the artist Dan Robbins and made artists out of anyone who could fill in the numbered and jigsawed spaces of their manufactured masterpieces. By 1954, more than twelve million sets had been sold. In 1992, an exhibit entitled The Fortieth Anniversary of Paint-by-Number Paintings, held at the Bridgewater/Lustberg Gallery in New York City, showcased the 200-plus paint-by-numbers belonging to the collector Michael O'Donoghue, who observed, "A masterpiece is just ten thousand brush strokes."

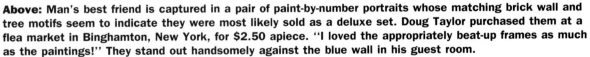

Above: Man's best friend is captured in a pair of paint-by-number portraits whose matching brick wall and tree motifs seem to indicate they were most likely sold as a deluxe set. Doug Taylor purchased them at a flea market in Binghamton, New York, for $2.50 apiece. "I loved the appropriately beat-up frames as much as the paintings!" They stand out handsomely against the blue wall in his guest room.

Left: Another "pet" project (also seen at far left) was secured more recently at Ruby Beets in Bridgehampton, New York, for $10.

Opposite, top: At the height of the paint-by-number craze, Craft Master produced up to 50,000 kits a day. Which is to say, there is no scarcity of these fill-in-the-blanks masterpieces. The three lined up on the mantelpiece in my carriage-house atelier in upstate New York were picked up at various tag sales for a quarter apiece.

Opposite, bottom: A trio of sporting scenes, all discovered at the Watnot Shop in Hudson, New York, for under $10 in 1986, appear to be the handiwork of one artist. They hang in our older son's bedroom in the country.

Sportsmen at heart are the collectors whose paintings are shown on these pages. Though not active participants in the games represented, the collectors find something about scenes of hearty souls standing in icy streams with poles poised or of a perfect speckled trout or antlered stag that stirs them toward another sport—hunting junk masters.

Clockwise from far left: Happy hunting grounds for wildlife art—the Twenty-sixth Street flea market in New York City, where the fisherman's paradise, seen in my office on Madison Avenue, above my old rolltop desk, was found. The painting cost $15. To the right, in our farmhouse office, flows an oil-on-canvas waterfall past a little wooden cabin, found in a barn for $35. To the right of it is a watercolor on paper of a swimming hole in Copake, New York. It cost a quarter at a garage sale nearby. Below it, in a farmhouse hallway, three varieties of game commingle—a hooked rug of fish found in an antiques shop in Millbrook, New York, for $50; a wooden articulated goose, a house gift from friends from Florida; and a mighty stag in a gilt frame, bought with the one seen on page 147 for $50 in Long Island. To the left, over the cluttered drawing board of an interior designer in Los Angeles, hangs a wooded landscape—the solitude he'd like to escape to—found in a flea market in Pasadena for $8. Next on the left is a prize catch from a London flea market—a watercolored speckled trout, one of a pair, purchased in a downpour for $65. At the far left, an "Indian love call" painted on black velvet cost $125, because, I was told, "It's quite an early one." Next to it is a homemade gun rack with a portrait, one suspects, of the donator of the antlers, bought for $35. The booty awaits a ride home (along with other finds) outside Flying Duck Outdoor Sporting Collectibles, the store where it was purchased, in Stuyvesant, New York.

At Ruby Beets in Bridgehampton, New York, many artistic themes, as well as media, are displayed together. The blond lady's head on a box with flowers cost $12. The Dutch-looking landscape under the flying fish, to the right of the Coca-Cola tray, cost $30. The fishermen in the boat to the far right (resembling a Marsden Hartley) cost $45. Sorry, they've been sold, but there's more where they came from.

Clockwise from top left: Thanks to van Gogh, Matisse, Bonnard, Vuillard, Renoir—you know the list—I have this soft spot for collecting paintings of flowers. Most of them, seen on these pages, hang in our farmhouse in upstate New York. The sunflowers, seen at the top left, were bought from Big John, the tall gentleman holding them in the doorway of his establishment—Big John's in San Francisco. The painting cost $8 and is framed in plastic. The challenge was getting it back to New York to hang it among the tools in our carriage house, seen to the right. The three florals temporarily on view in our New York City living room were purchased at the Twenty-sixth Street flea market early one Saturday. The one on the top cost $75. The other two cost $50 apiece. (To see them in their eventual home, see pages 154–155.) To the right is a vase of flowers, heavily laden with pigment (see detail below), which I bought last summer at Parker's Trading Post in Elizabeth City, North Carolina. For fun we set it up one day on the dunes outside our cottage. The whole thing, including the extraordinary frame and the easel, cost $25. To the left of the close-up, under the three florals, is another, much more primitive, vase of flowers hanging in our country dining room. It came from a thrift shop in Hudson, New York (where it is seen below), for $10. The little rose painting, picked up at a country Grange hall tag sale and photographed there, cost, as you can see, $4.50. Above it, on another wallpapered room in our country house, is one of my favorite still lifes, bought in a shop in Connecticut for $16. It was painted by Ann Spiro in 1949.

Rescuing Junk Masterpieces

I must admit to doing very little to the hundreds of paintings I've collected in the last ten years. When you're spending $10, $20, or even $50, you can't expect a painting to be in perfect condition. Enjoy them for what they are—original pieces of art. I love the charm of a little grime ("patina," I call it!) on my paintings. But even I occasionally try to brighten up what my husband, Howard, calls my "dark paintings." Below are some ideas on how to go about it, plus how to deal with rips and tears and some general cosmetic improvers, provided by Pat Carter, my mother, whose collection inspired mine, and Alice Reid, a good friend and antiques dealer from Livingston, New York, who both strongly advise, "Proceed with our suggestions at your own risk!"

- "In general," warns Alice, "don't do too much. Most paintings are pretty fragile. If you must, barely dampen a soft cloth and try to lightly remove surface dust and grime with it. Sometimes I dip my cloth into a diluted mixture of Ivory Snow and warm water. Make sure you don't wet the canvas. Chances are the water will soak through and spot the back of it. Too much soap and water will dry out and crack the pigments. "<u>Don't</u>," says Alice, "use Fantastik or any other spray cleaner on an old painting."

- One way to "dry clean" an oil painting is my mother's Wonder bread method. Ball up very fresh Wonder bread slices into doughy little pellets. Rub one at a time gently over the surface of the painting. The dough balls crumble, so to prevent an even bigger mess, spread newspaper under the project. (Alice reports that she's heard of this technique being used to clean up old wallpaper.)

- Changing a frame can make a big difference in the way a painting looks. "Sometimes the frames are so tacky, or too ornate for the art work," concedes my mother. "Adding a mat can also improve a junk masterpiece," she suggests. She cuts her own out of sheets of high-quality drawing paper.

- To repair a small tear or rip (I say, "Why bother?"), Alice suggests a couple of tricks. Duct tape on the back of the painting, behind the tear, should help it cosmetically and also help to prevent further damage. A fine piece of linen attached with Elmer's glue on the back, over the tear, can work. "Make sure you tuck in the frayed edges," warns Alice, "so everything dries flat."

- My mother has been known to touch up a painting with Magic Markers or crayons. For watercolors, try Caran d'Ache, Swiss-made crayons that, when dipped in water, give a watercolor effect.

She's English. He's French. The apartment they share in New York City is long and skinny, minimally furnished with just a few overstuffed chairs, a sofa, a nineteenth-century French chaise longue, and three cats named Henri, Coco, and Baby. (Their five other felines can be seen on pages 118–119.) The walls reflect less restraint, totally surrendered to the couple's mutual passion for the visual arts. Volumes of oversized art and photography books, seen on the following pages, are neatly stacked on floor-to-ceiling shelves built especially to accommodate them. An impressive black-and-white photography collection has long since outgrown similar accommodations. Between the two collections, above topiaries and a treasured marble mantel, seen at right, is displayed yet a third collection—paintings, mostly still lifes, collected by the lady of the house. Inspired a decade ago by an exhibition of Italian Renaissance still-life paintings, the owner set off to collect her own (cheaper) versions. The most expensive, at $400, hangs in the center, directly over the mantel. It was discovered in a tiny shop in Paris. The chalky pastel above it was a gift from "him." The rather Cubist still life to its right is French, found in Tangier. (If you look carefully you will discover photographs of our art-loving couple, Didier Malige and Grace Coddington, among the minutiae of the mantelpiece.

Above: The room at the top of the stairs, above the collections seen at left and on the following pages, is cozy—tucked under the eaves—white, and sublimely understated. Sunlight streams in from French doors that open to a rooftop garden, the real home of the topiary at right. It warms the top of an old green blanket chest next to the bed, with its beautifully carved Mexican headboard. On the chest is a portrait of a lady from the 1940s, bought in a shop a few blocks away for $100. The leopard-skin hat by Chanel is a new one that looks as though it just came off the lady behind it. The unopened package is from Paris—new books to be added to the collection downstairs.

Following pages: A Cinemascope look at the wall housing the above-the-mantelpiece exhibit of paintings at left reveals two more staggering collections. At the right, a stylish gallery of images by Jacques-Henri Lartigue, Karsh, Bruce Weber, Louise Dahl-Wolfe, Horst, Lee Miller, Sheila Metzner, Cecil Beaton, and others lines not only the shelves but the floor below. To the left, oversized volumes of art and photography books are cleverly accommodated by rows of shelves designed for easy access and great aesthetics.

shady business

Robert Miller, a New York art dealer, loves shaded lamps "for the intimate patches of light they create." Judyth vanAmringe, a creator of shades that look like hats (see her Easter parade of them on the previous pages), loves their innate sense of humor. Both would agree that lamp shades build character in the rooms they inhabit. (Witness how spineless the lamp at right becomes when stripped of its precious individuality.) No collector on the next thirteen pages would be caught dead with an overhead fluorescent light in his or her home!

Above: Posing in the window of U.S.E.D., a New York City home to born-again treasures, is a ruffled-lady lamp from the fifties —later sold for $85.

Left: A real odd couple of shades bought together at a tag sale for a quarter. I loved the straightforwardness of the green plastic one, sewed together by some hardworking soul. The pink pleated one tucked below it made me think of an opposite-side-of-the-tracks kind of love story. It was a totally sentimental purchase.

Previous pages: Surrounded by the friendly clutter of chintz chairs, long-legged egrets, picture frames, books, you name it, is a family of lamps decked out in the most amazing headgear. "I was a hat designer first," admits Judyth vanAmringe. All her shades are silk; some are old, some are new, but all have been tampered with. Living proof: the flowery shade in the center, bursting with yellow pansies. "It was a hat originally," confesses the designer. On top of the yellow poodle to the right is a signature vanAmringe shade. Originally silk, and badly frayed when Judyth found it, it was subsequently coated with a heavy application of gesso, creating a canvas for the artist's originality. A new silk shade (Judyth's design), painted and fringed, stands tall in front of it. The little skirted shade to the right of the poodle is another whimsy she came up with. (Don't fall in love with what you see here. Most likely, someone else already did.)

Far left: Lamp shades build character, to which the skeletal remains of the one clinging to this undernourished lamp at Pink Paraffin—a secondhander's paradise in San Francisco—attests. I passed on it in favor of the $22 magazine rack side table (in the pink of condition!) underneath (see it in its new home 3,000 miles away on page 151).

Above: Hard times had befallen this young Victorian flower girl, a plaster lamp with a yellowed silk shade, as seen up for sale for $20 at The Joneses, a landmark junk shop in Great Barrington, Massachusetts.

Left: Happy at last, our maiden was bought by a sympathetic couple (my husband and me) and removed to our farmhouse nearby.

How to Clean an Old Silk Lamp Shade: Tips from Judyth vanAmringe

The first rule is handle with care, since many old silk shades are incredibly sere. Start with a gentle dusting with a barely damp soft cloth or the smallest brush attachment from a vacuum cleaner. If you wish to go further, shades can be dunked in a warm bath of Ivory Snow flakes. Swish them around in it and avoid scrubbing. Rinse with cold water and hang outside to dry. A wet shade must dry fast or else its metal frame will rust. If drying outside is impossible, try your hair dryer. If a shade is beyond cleaning, use it as a canvas for creating fresh, new designs. Judyth uses acrylic paints. They don't fade and they're waterproof.

A P.S. on parchment shades—wash the exterior with "dry" top suds and a wrung-out sponge. Wipe off the suds with a clean damp sponge or cloth and, working quickly, dry the surface. Repeat on interior.

Sharone Einhorn, the founder of Ruby Beets, a store in Bridgehampton, New York, which is set up like a house furnished with faded old chintz chairs and painted furniture, has a secret. It's her own house (the one she doesn't get to very often, now that her business is booming). Tucked behind an overgrown hedgerow in a nearby village, it's every bit as great as her store, except it doesn't get bought up every weekend. See its entrance above, the garden shed below, and more on pages 74–75.

Left: Without question, it is the pair of fringed silk Victorian lamp shades balanced on top of marble-based, fluted brass columns that transforms Sharone Einhorn's spartan bedroom into something on the order of Miss Havisham's boudoir in <u>Great Expectations</u>. In fact, as they rest on an old wooden toolbox, which Sharone dry brushed with latex paint, one can almost see the cobwebs forming. Sharone found them in a Victorian house (where else?) and admits to paying dearly ($275) for the pair. She expects they date from 1910, and though she tends to dislike brass, found these lamps acceptable due to their pitted condition. The damask tea towel, piled with bedside reading and a pink alarm clock from Caldor's, drapes toward one of a pair of pastel-striped rag rugs she found in Saratoga Springs for $75. Other bedside necessities: a trim-line phone and a biography of Anne Sexton.

Above: Signs of life abound in Sharone's under-the-eaves bedroom. In the window at right, Widget, her half-Burmese cat from Spanish Harlem, having just watched her mistress's departure, goes on with her grooming. A towel hastily thrown over the armchair assumes the casual elegance of a decorator throw. The chambray work shirt dropped on the crocheted bedspread, however, does not. The simple romance of the room—heightened by the white painted floors, bedspread, Victorian fringed tie-back curtains, the pair of fringed silk lamps, and floral touches on the faded chintz armchair, dust ruffle, and little hooked rug—stands in stark contrast to the modern look of the three-legged chair seen under the window. Designated as one of her better finds—"from a junk yard"—the chair is made of copper tubing and cushioned by Sharone with a pillow stapled with old fabric.

Above: On a junking expedition in upstate New York, my sister Liza and I simultaneously spied a Grandma Moses kind of painted bottle lamp in a shop we frequently haunt. She got there first and claimed it.

Right: Liza's lamp was claimed in turn by her four-year-old son, John, who placed it next to his bed in New York City. To shade it, Liza covered a dime-store-variety lamp shade with crinkly gauze. She sewed the gathered edge, at the top, right through the frame; the lower edge, which hangs about an inch longer than the shade when gathered taut, disappears inside the shade. The quality of the light is very gentle and at night illuminates the bedside treasures of this "junker-in-training," as his proud mother calls John. The ceramic dog ashtray to the right was picked up by both of them at the Twenty-sixth Street flea market in New York for $2. John loved "the doggy," Liza "the mock majolica." The little green box next to it with a decoupaged squirrel on top was $4. John stores secret things in it. Nuts, perhaps? A decoupaged tray (the edge of which is seen to the left of the lamp) holds a pottery candlestick, a school project made by John's sister, Mary Randolph. The bright, folksy painting behind it, a contribution from Liza, was discovered on a subway ride. She saw it in the hands of a woman who turned out to be the artist. A sale was transacted on the spot. The hand-tinted photograph of the little boy in blue pushing his wheelbarrow is signed and dated 1909. Liza squealed with delight when she found it in a shop in Richmond. The child bears a striking resemblance to her son. It was a treasure at any price; she paid $3.

Above: The interior and wheels of this Lilliputian-sized covered-wagon night light (measuring 6″ long) was handcrafted from a cactus skeleton. I picked it up for a couple of dollars at the annual Millerton, New York, Grange flea market.

Left: Though she won't swear to it, Liza Carter Norton, the discoverer of this caramel-colored marble-based lamp (in a shop in New Jersey), believes the transparent shell squares pieced into the brass grid of the shade to be abalone. She feels the $30 she invested in it was money "well spent." The intricately carved wooden piece in front of it she bought at a street fair in Hong Kong for $10. "It's a gilded panel out of a door or room divider, I'm positive." The couple on either side of the lamp, dressed in native costume (no clue as to their country of origin), are painted plaster. I bought them in a junk shop in Richmond, Virginia, on a visit home, and gave them to Liza one Christmas. It wouldn't be fair to reveal the price, but suffice it to say they were a bargain. So was the majolica plate in the foreground at right. "Ten dollars for it, and half that for the green earthenware bowl behind it," quotes Liza. "The plastic fruit I collected piece by piece at an average of 50 cents. The oil painting on the wall behind it is in another category, a gift from Mother." The curtains are the only thing new in the picture.

Right: "Necessity is the mother of invention" was never more keenly demonstrated than with the old homemade bottle lamp found for $12 by Sam and Gloria Landers at the Franklin Flea and Craft Market, which they frequent on weekends in Franklin, North Carolina. The shade—a red straw fruit basket overturned and fringed with red-and-white pom-poms, makes this homemade piece of wizardry a recycled treasure.

Above: As seen on the porch of the Landers's mountain getaway, a warm glow streams through the slats of this red basket lamp shade.

Left: In Robert and Betsy Miller's Miami Beach wonderland of lamps (see more on the following pages), this lamp shade stands out as a masterpiece of utilitarian ingenuity. A conventional straw waste basket, turned upside down, has been given new life as a lighthearted shade for a floor lamp, rescued from a local Miami Beach thrift shop for $10, which now inhabits the hallway of their sunny Florida home. The Millers applaud the lamp's unknown innovator.

Robert Miller is drawn to lamps—lots of them, as the next few photos will attest. The lamps (upward of thirty) scattered around the Miami Beach duplex he shares with his wife, Betsy, and their three teenaged children were all found in neighborhood thrift shops for less than $20 each. Most of them tend to be from the forties and fifties, when laced-to-the-frame fiberglass shades were de rigueur. The one above, seen in the master bedroom, is a masterpiece. On each panel is glued a flowery still life made of bits of colored glass. The base is solid mahogany.

"Lamps, for me," confesses Robert Miller, "are about mood and softness. The tints of the bulbs, the colors of the shades create intimate patches of light." The lamp in the living room, standing behind a particularly comfortable chair, is turned on to read by. "It's adjustable, allows good light over the shoulder, and the wood matches the furniture. What more could you ask for?"

In what must be the most arid corner of the Millers' living room, there is assembled on top of a painted wooden pedestal table the dried-out remains of seaweed fragments shoved in paled yellow glasses. More suited to this desert environment is the plaster cactus-shaped lamp rising in the center, topped by a fiberglass shade the color of Key lime pie. The bamboo screen behind it was designed especially for the apartment.

On top of the baby grand, swathed with a bumpy chenille bedspread (to protect it from moisture, more than from the objects cluttered on top of it; see pages 222–223), rises a slightly dented, slightly skewed pewter lamp stuck with random globs of amber, probably a department-store Chinese import from the twenties, posits the resident master of lamps—Robert Miller. The shade, a naturalist prize, preserves stems of flowers and grasses between diaphanous layers of laced-together fiberglass.

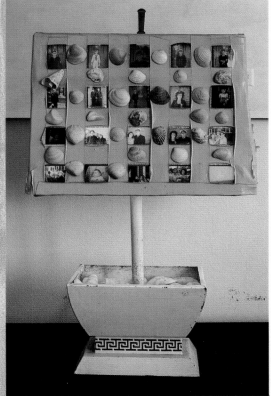

Above: On the bedside table in Robert and Betsy Miller's guest room in Miami Beach, there are no books or magazines to be seen. There's no TV or radio, either. The most intriguing entertainment source is provided by the lone lamp, covered by a remarkable photo-album lamp shade. "When someone turns on the light they can read a novel or create their own script for a sentimental home movie with these images," suggests Mr. Miller. The photographic transparencies, woven into a gridlike storyboard (see detail at left) with yellowing masking tape and accented with shells, are reminiscent of a <u>Winds of War</u> kind of mini-series, based on a real seafaring family, probably stationed in Florida in the forties. It was a present to the Millers from Roberto Juarez, "a close friend and great artist." He found the lamp in the Douglas Garden Thrift Store in northwest Miami.

shell shocked

Shells could be the purest form of junk. (They're certainly the cleanest.) They're the ocean's refuse—the discarded packaging of more than 75,000 kinds of invertebrates. Shell seekers date back to the sixteenth and seventeenth centuries. Some sought the individual rare specimen; others chose to amass large collections to cluster in niches and along the borders of or-

nate shell rooms. The real shell wampum of today comes from what was the souvenir mania of Miami Beach in the thirties. No self-respecting tourist could go home without at least one pair of shell-encrusted salt and pepper shakers, a shell frame, or a carved cowrie.

Above: A shell stew of fragments and shards served up in an old enamel washbasin at Pontes Antiques in Kill Devil Hills, North Carolina.

Above left: The Humpty-Dumpty remains of conch shells piled into a driftwood ''duck'' box handcrafted by Outer Banks artist Charles Reber.

Above: Scattered across the surface of Sharone Einhorn's marble-topped dressing table in Sag Harbor, New York, is what you might expect to find in a seaside bedroom —odd pieces of shell, bone, a holey piece of driftwood, and a five-fingered bud vase that looks like branches of white coral. Less expected is the Hindu clay statue Sharone discovered in a shop in New York City for $150.

Right: Bridget O'Neill, the fourteen-year-old daughter of Ellen (whose homes we have visited on pages 97–105), occupies this spartan white bedroom on the eastern end of Long Island during summers and holidays. The only extraneous decoration is a piece of white coral, a gift from her friends at Blooming Shells, a shop in Sag Harbor. The lantern, which is wired, came from another local haunt, Sage Street Antiques, for $9. The mirror with "that fun-house kind of glass in it that distorts everything," Bridget moans, was found in Brimfield, Massachusetts, for $14.

Above: The little shell sewing kit found at Ruby Beets for $10 was probably a souvenir brought back from Florida in the forties. I gave it to my eight-year-old goddaughter and niece, Mary Randolph, who keeps it filled with her own prized shell collection. She swears that if she lifts the lid gently, she can hear the sound of the ocean.

Following pages: A close examination of my son Sam's summer desktop reveals new acquisitions—mostly conchs (his specialty), plus a crab shell, an unidentified crustacean next to it, and a good hunk of fossilized sand embedded with seaweed and scallop shells. On top of a jar of buttons, bought for $3 (perhaps in hopes of discovering some made of pearl and mollusk), is a calcified shell that looks like a claw. The bound volumes of <u>Scientific American</u>, a resource for more marine-life data, he hopes, were my contribution from an auction in Kitty Hawk, North Carolina—three bound volumes for $1. The movie camera above them, a $5 auction item, and its leather case, handy for transporting an inventory of fragile scallop and mollusk samples, went to Sam. The miniature set of Golden encyclopedias, seven volumes for $5, included one on fish (opened below the camera case) and another on shells. The legionnaire's cap, upper right, was sent by a caring aunt, who found it in a New York City flea market for $2. He has promised to wear it on midday beach foraging expeditions.

Above: To flavor any kitchen table—a pair of tiny shell-encrusted salt and pepper shakers, souvenirs of Miami from the forties. It's hard to tell if these were store bought or created by bored vacationers on a rainy day. If you're totally obsessed (as I am) with these shell shakers and can't find anything close, follow the directions below, borrowed from the wonderful little shell-craft volume <u>Fun with Shells</u>, by Joseph Leeming, published in 1958, and make your own.

Make Your Own Shell Shakers

Start with plain glass shakers with colored plastic tops, which can be obtained at any discount store. Cover the sides of the shaker with a quarter-inch coating of putty or gesso, using a table knife to spread it on. Then press different kinds of small shells into it until the whole shaker is covered. When the putty has hardened, apply a coat of clear lacquer. You can use any small shells, such as coquinas and small clam shells.

Right: "What really turned me on to shell stuff," admits Doug Taylor, the proprietor of Praiseworthy Antiques in Guilford, New York, "is that it was the first real tourist junk in Florida. It was very home-crafty— basically, shells-set-in-clay kind of stuff." A perfect example is his shell frame encircling a Rubenesque beauty—a postcard stand-in, marked $3. As for the frame, "We're talking early, early Miami Beach," puts in Doug. It cost him less than $10.

On the large shell, an inscription reads:

"
Call us not weeds
We are flowers of the sea
For lovely and bright
And gay tinted are we
And quite independent—
Of sunshine or showers
Then call us not weeds
We are oceans gay flowers
"

Above: Doug Taylor can recite by heart the little ode to seaweed inscribed on what he calls "the ultimate flea market find ever!" Inside, nestled one on top of another, are twenty parchment pages onto which are pressed miniature specimens of dried seaweed—"from Cape Cod," he thinks. The collection of carved cowries surrounding it—the earliest dating from the 1800s—is a form of souvenir found worldwide. The one at the lower right has the Lord's Prayer carved on top; the one above it inscribed in Hebrew is from Israel. All were found at "random junk sales" for "a dollar or two."

Left: The two shell jars on the back row, center and right, were found by my sister Liza and me. (We gave them to each other, so we can't reveal the prices!) The one in the back row, left, was inspired by these, and made as a beach project last summer. It's a peanut butter jar smeared with gesso and stuck-in shells. The two in the front row, a clay-based vase and a miniature sewing kit, were $1 at a tag sale.

Right: A tiny white moon follows the course of a romantic old inky-green ocean liner as it passes through the deep mid-night-blue night, the same color as the water. Inside the ship, there are glamorous people dancing to the music of Benny Goodman. The ghostly trail of smoke pouring out of the ship's triple stacks looks like a surreal hand about to grab it. Over the boat shines one bright star, "which particularly drew me to it," explains the owner, Judyth vanAmringe (see pages 70–71, 132–133, and 136–137), an artist and dealer in magical finds like this, which she bought in Maine for $65. The starfish were a gift received the same week. The protruding frame allowed for their installation. "I love the touch of 3-D they bring."

Below: The star box, as it is known by the Miller family, sometimes holds tissues in the downstairs powder room. Sometimes, it holds an orchid, as it did when Betsy Miller's sister-in-law, Jennifer, presented it to her after a birthday party she gave in Hobe Sound, Florida. Encrusted with starfish, shells, little seahorses, and bright sand, it made a remarkable centerpiece on the party table. "From Hobe Sound to Miami Beach," where it now resides in the Millers' oceanside apartment, "is a distance of light-years," remarks Betsy's husband, Robert, a New York art dealer, with a smile. The petal table it rests on came from a shop in South Beach that has since been leveled by a developer. It dates from the late forties, and cost $10.

Left: You might mistake Vanity Novelty Garden, a bright blue storefront in South Miami Beach with two large orange fish over the door, for a local fish market. Tamara Hendershot, the proprietor, will sell you a fish of the sort seen in this picture, but nothing fresh. Outline the fish you desire on a painted board, glue in shells, sprinkle a little aquarium sand along the bottom, add a piece of seaweed for dimension, and you can have one like this, which cost its owner $15, for free!

Below: On the second floor of the Millers' Miami Beach duplex, there's an interior bedroom window that looks down on the living room and out to the ocean. A fifties ceramic conch, a gift from a friend and colleague of Bob's, always sits there. The sportsman's trophies floating behind it were probably caught in the Gulf Stream right outside the window above them.

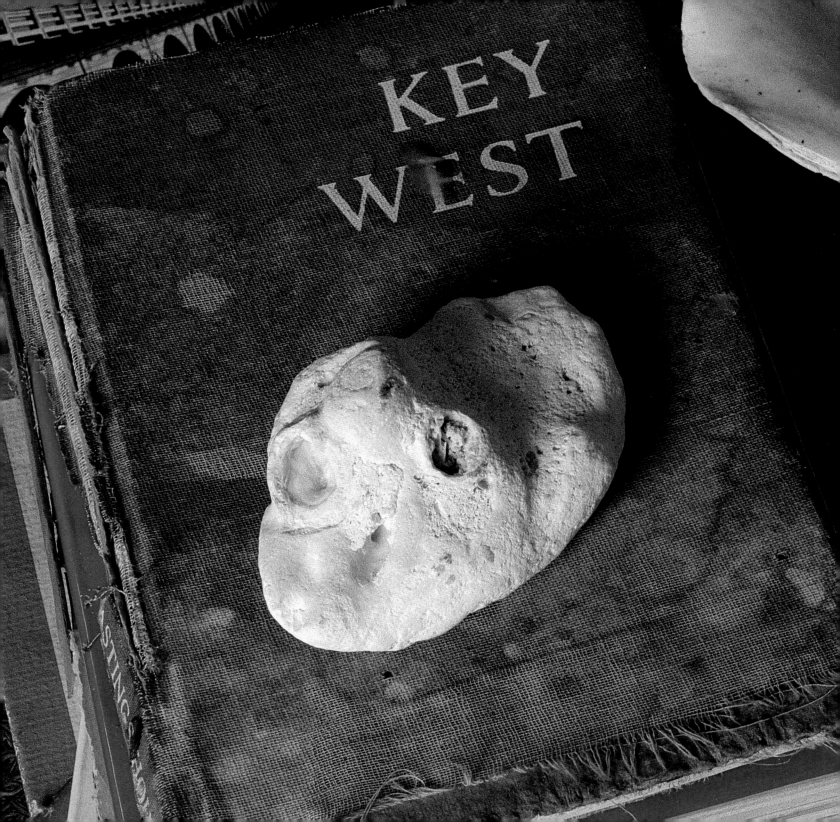

If visitors didn't know better, they might think the river below Richard Giglio's New York City penthouse terrace (see pages 77—81) had risen fifteen stories and swept through his apartment, leaving shells and coral fragments strewn all over. Not so. The large clam shell at right, a memento from his second home, Key West, is used as a bowl for fruits and vegetables. The coral piece at left rests on a book about Key West, circa 1940, which looks as though it might have survived a few high tides of its own.

heavy metal

In the 1930s, photographer Margaret Bourke-White saw an America where "Dynamos are more beautiful . . . than pearls. The beauty of industry lies within its truth and simplicity: every line is essential, therefore beautiful." Would she have paused at the shelf at left, in a secondhand emporium in upstate New York, displaying tributes to domestic industry—an electrified coffee urn, a stainless steel thermos, and a silver teapot? Perhaps not, but, thinking of a friend of mine, another photographer with a sensibility not unlike Margaret Bourke-White's, I did, and purchased the thermos and another for less than $10 apiece for her. (See the pair on the following pages.) Two years later, I walked into Stuart Parr's showroom loft in lower Manhattan and spied a gleaming 1936 Waterwitch outboard motor housed in polished aluminum and mounted like a modernist sculpture. I gave it to my husband, Howard, for his birthday. "Does it work?" he asked. (For more on how that went, see page 204.) In the movies, Lora Zarubin, a collector of (among other things) objects of tin, would have met the Tin Man in The Wizard of Oz. In the real world, she is quite content with a galvanized tin stool and a bathroom full of hammered tin religious amulets called milagros (see page 206). If you should ask for a cup of tea at Robert and Betsy Miller's home in Miami Beach, you will discover the perfect metal teapot work of art. When not in use, it resides on the top of their Whirlpool stove, set off by four coiled burners that remind one (in the Millers' art-intense environment) of mobiles by Alexander Calder.

Left: Though it shares a similar job description with the silver coffee urn and teapot it stood between at a secondhand emporium in upstate New York, this stainless steel thermos from the fifties has a streamlined simplicity that sets it immediately apart.

Following pages: The thermos and a smaller ribbed version, bought for $14, were gifts to my friend Brigitte Lacombe, the photographer, who gave them a new kind of dignity by displaying them on industrial shelving filled with art and design books and her black-and-white portraits of writer David Mamet, at left, and Bernardo Bertolucci with actor John Malkovich.

I'm not sure when my husband, Howard, started his transportation collection. His guess is 1974, provoked by my relentless pursuit of a hundred different collections at weekend flea markets. The outboard motor at right, a 1936 Waterwitch, is his latest prize—a birthday present from me.

I spied the polished aluminum housing gleaming among the twentieth-century decorative arts assembled by dealer and collector Stuart Parr in his showroom/loft in New York City. Outboard motors like the Waterwitch are not easily found, but if you come across one you can probably get it fairly reasonably. Clean it up, mount it, or hang it from a wall. P.S. It doesn't work, but according to Stuart it wouldn't take much to make it work.

Above and right: Industrial designers of the thirties took great pride in turning utilitarian machines like this 1936 aluminum and steel Waterwitch outboard motor, manufactured by Sears, Roebuck and Company, into machine-age sculpture.

Above and left: Brigitte Lacombe came to New York City about twelve years ago. Very quickly she established herself as a photographer whose portraits of well-known people revealed something largely unknown about them before. She has never relied on props or fashion, but instead has focused her camera directly on character. The large black-and-white portrait, at left, of Isabella Rossellini is proof enough. The classic aluminum chair in front of it is indicative of her similar pared-down approach to decorating. She found it discarded on a street (see above) not far from her apartment. A tag on the bottom of the seat says it was manufactured in 1951, under the name "Good Form," by the General Fireproofing Company in Youngstown, Ohio. The tag also suggests cleaning with Wright's silver cream. A good substitute (since Wright's is no longer available) is Nevr-Dull polish. It cleans and polishes all metals, including silver, gold, brass, copper, pewter, steel, aluminum, and chromium. The wadding, soaked with a cleaning solution, comes rolled in a can. You tear off a piece and rub the article until it's clean. For a great shine, buff with a dry soft cloth. A five-ounce can runs about $3 at most hardware stores.

ora Zarubin's restaurant—
LORA—on West Thirteenth
Street in New York City has a
little green-and-white primitive cupboard, found at a flea
market, on the wall of the ladies'
room. It, like the little red metal
desk lamp from the thirties that
lights up the reservation list in the
evening (from a shop in western
Connecticut), the starburst-like
crystal chandelier floating over
the old zinc bar in the restaurant's
foyer (both found in Paris flea
markets), and the collection of
primitive American paintings of
fruit compotes, three of which
lean against the dining-room wall
on a shelf over stacks of freshly
baked rounds of bread, are
among the rare and homey
touches (not unlike the condi-
ments in her cooking) that are offered to those who come to
"Lora's" table. It is not surprising
that Lora's <u>other</u> home (for really,
the restaurant is her home as
well), in a beautiful apartment
house built in the thirties and
shared with Nino, her faithful
wire-haired fox terrier, is filled
with the same kind of special and
unusual touches.

Opposite, far left: Hanging on the wall of Lora's bathroom at home is a collection of <u>milagros</u>, religious amulets from as early as the turn of the century, made of thin hammered tin or silver in the shape of parts of the body. Catholics from Italy and Mexico relied on them to help cure everything from a runny nose to heart disease. A <u>milagro</u> in the form of the ailing part of the anatomy—ear, lungs, hand, foot, nose—was taken to the local church and hung on a statue of the saint to which the supplicant prayed. The saint was then implored to bring his or her healing powers to bear on behalf of the petitioner or a friend or family member. Lora's first <u>milagro</u>, received years back when she lived in San Francisco, was a gift from an artist friend. "I know for a fact it cost just a few dollars. Since then, I must admit to spending a lot more on them." Though she says she didn't really think about it, their place next to the medicine cabinet seems appropriate. "Unfortunately, the steam from the shower is forever tarnishing them, but I love the implied relationship to the body."

Left: In the last few years, Lora made the decision to minimize the possessions around her. She wanted each room to have less, so the focus could be on one or two special pieces. In her bedroom, one of those pieces is definitely the galvanized tin stool she uses as a night table. "It's from the twenties or thirties, from that great dairy state, Wisconsin" (though she bought it from a friend who bought it in a shop in East Hampton, New York.) Set in her all-white bedroom, topped with a Bernice black lamp and a contemporary alarm clock, the rustic stool takes on a modern sculptural attitude. The photograph of three apples behind it, taken by a friend, Barbara Wyeth, from San Francisco, shares that same spirit.

Above: Brigitte Lacombe retrieved this large pewter vase not too many summers ago from the attic of her family's summer home in the south of France. She decided to bring it back to her favorite room with all the memories rubbed deep into its tarnished old finish.

The Gift of Junk:
A True Story

This past Christmas my mother let each of us children and our spouses draw a number. In order—1 to 15—we were allowed to go to the barn (the holding tank for our large family's collective lost and abandoned treasures) and choose something as our present. We each took our turn (I was #9) and ran back in to share with the rest what we had chosen. My brother Jimmie (he got #1) went for a set of six old leaded-glass windows. My sister Clelland (#4) found an old set of dishes with blue grapes painted on them. I found an old green coffee table that Mother had fixed up when I was six. We couldn't fit it in the car, but my number's on it. "Don't wait too long," warns a sister (#10) who's got her eye on it.

Left: With its home on the range (in Betsy and Robert Miller's Miami Beach kitchen—for more see pages 184–187 and 222–225), this old pewter teapot takes on sculptural dimensions, set off by the Calder-like coiled heating burners. Collected from a neighborhood thrift shop for a couple of dollars, "it's quite functional still," reports its frequent handler, Mr. Miller. "The wicker-wrapped handle and wooden top showed a good deal of common sense on the part of the designer" (unknown).

chair crazy

In the category of furniture, chairs offer the best opportunity for inexpensive self-expression. At $1, which is what was paid for the rocker at right, they're absolutely irresistible. The splintery spindle-back on the opposite page was five times that—still a bargain, considering it's signed. (Inspect its back rail closely on pages 214–215.) A great-looking chair can be hung on the wall (Shaker style), be displayed on top of a piano (Think I'm kidding? See pages 222–223), or used for stacks of books and magazines.

Previous pages: Silhouetted against the window of what was the original hayloft of our carriage house in upstate New York is the $1 rocking chair seen opposite. After a hard day of junking, it is the perfect seat from which to view not only the landscape but the prizes of the day scattered around it.

Far left: The details that absolutely charmed me about this little wooden rocker so lovingly restored by some very romantic, yet very precise, amateur decorator were the machine-embroidered flowered satin fabric on the back and the blue thumbtacks pressed in at two- and three-inch intervals around the outer edges. Set off by a blue-gray paint (chipped in spots, revealing a plainer wood color beneath), it probably once rocked in a bedroom just as dainty. More painstaking care is revealed on the other side of the chair (seen on the previous pages in our carriage-house loft) —a panel of the machine-embroidered peonies perfectly set off by the frame of the chair's back. All this for a dollar at Michael Fallon's Copake Country Auction in Copake, New York.

Left: Ellen O'Neill's $5 chair was quickly scooped up in front of a store in Sag Harbor, New York. It's dated and signed—as the close-up of the top rail attests to very clearly on the next page. "It's very splintery," reports Ellen, but very sturdy. The pinprick holes speckled about reveal that it is also quite appetizing to uninvited guests —wood fleas, more than likely. The 1940s straw hat encircled with a brown rayon band reminds Ellen of the one Ingrid Bergman wore in <u>Casablanca</u> when she was leaving on the plane in the last scene. It was a gift from an "extravagant" friend, who spent $20 for it.

A close-up of vintage graffiti carved on the top rail of Ellen O'Neill's "splintery" chair, seen on the previous pages.

Right: According to my sister Nell, who found this wicker chair (with the flowers intact) and four others in brown—the lot: $125—in a shop near Williamsburg, Virginia, they are supposedly "pub chairs from England." The pink one has taken a radical turn—enough to warrant placing it in her six-year-old daughter's un-publike bedroom. The colorful circular rug beneath it cost $5, at Cecil's in Richmond, Virginia. Framed above it is a Carl Larsson poster.

Right: Richard Giglio's eighteenth-century Venetian chair is a fake. He bought the frame for $150, new, twenty years ago from a furniture maker in New York City. The silver leaf, applied then, now looks gold. The floral remnant draped over the seat is a French chintz from the thirties, a gift, with several others, from Rose Cumming, a legendary antiques dealer in New York City. The oversized pillow on the back was another "sort-of-gift" from a friend who wanted to "unload" it and three others. (More on Giglio's style on pages 77–81.)

Above: I bought this rather fussy upholstered armchair slipcovered in what looks like French toile de Jouy as kind of a joke, because it came so close to matching the red-and-white paper on the walls in our farmhouse parlor. (Two years later, we stripped off the wallpaper and painted the walls white—now the joke's on us, because the chair is so comfortable it's not going anywhere!) It came from Johnson and Johnson Antiques (see following pages) for $50. The daisy pillow in the center is an oversized pincushion from the 1930s that cost 50 cents at a yard sale. Flanking it are two Log Cabin quilt patch pillows (very old), bought more than ten years ago at a flea market in Connecticut for $5 apiece.

Left: In Ellen's upstairs bathroom, a child's Adirondack chair ($18, from Pennsylvania) provides a seat for extra towels. The $4 "popsicle-stick" stool (as she calls it) is for "kids who can't reach the sink." The vanity-table skirt with the quilted top romanticizing her sink was discovered years ago in a box lot of stuff for $2.

Above: In Ellen O'Neill's bathroom (off her kitchen) in Sag Harbor (see pages 98–101) resides a duo of slip-covered pretenders. The one on the right, seen fully in the picture at right, is not an upholstered armchair but actually a wooden lawn chair (bought at Sage Street Antiques in Sag Harbor for $12). Ellen paid $8 for the cabbage-rose slipcover at the Brimfield Market. Its sidekick to the left is "off its rocker," according to Ellen, which accounts for its lowness—a $6 find from William Doyle Gallery, New York City. Dressed up with another Brimfield slipcover, made from an old forties print she picked up for $20, it looks a little bit like a child dressed in her mother's clothes (see it again at the far right).

Laundering Tips

Ellen throws her old slipcovers into the washing machine. Use the gentle cycle with cold water. If you're fitting them on an upholstered chair, like the toile de Jouy one on the opposite page, let them air dry and pull them on the chair while still damp. If you're using them as Ellen does, to drape over a chair, this isn't necessary.

Right: The top floor of Johnson and Johnson Antiques in Millerton, New York, is like the best attic in the world, particularly if you're in search of chairs. It's also a little like a museum of tattered, frayed, slightly sagging, slightly wobbly chairs of all ages, shapes, and sizes. Bargains are in evidence, but prices are firm—no haggling. The American-made Eastlake folding armchair on the left is upholstered with carpetlike fabric. To the right is a rather undistinguished armchair upholstered with a rich-looking floral, totally wrecked at the back.

Old Chair Checkout

The main thing to check for when buying an old upholstered chair is to see if the bottom is falling out. Sharone Einhorn of Ruby Beets in Bridgehampton, New York, hunts down old armchairs on a weekly basis. "If the springs are coming out," she insists, "don't buy it!" On the other hand, if there's a bad stain on the back, "just back it up against a wall." Sharone makes a point of investigating what lies under upholstery (especially if it's awful). "Snip away and you may discover a beautiful old vintage fabric." If it's not there, she prefers to start over again with muslin upholstery and then slipcover the chair in vintage fabric. My favorite form of chair cosmetics is creatively draping an old shawl or blanket over offensive spots, holes, or lurid colors. My mother once transformed a lackluster armchair by upholstering it with a couple of old army blankets in less than two hours.

Above: "My favorite chair," says Ellen with a sigh, has an adjustable back ($18 at Sage Street) and a hyacinth-and-periwinkle pillow. Layered on the floor are Swedish bed rugs that cost $35 each. "I once pulled one over me on a cold night," recalls Ellen. "I felt like Laura Ingalls Wilder sleeping with a lead vest on!"

Top left: My pair of scalloped-backed garden chairs from the 1940s had been in antiques dealer Alice Reid's own backyard. Their rust-corroded bottoms are disguised with pillowcases.

Left: A child's blue metal yard chair from the 1940s cost Ellen O'Neill $10 at Sage Street Antiques in Sag Harbor.

Above: A primitive twig rocker found in Pennsylvania and "painted blue by someone else" was a "rather dear purchase at sixty-five dollars," Ellen admits. It was probably not intended for a visiting wire-haired fox terrier, but the O'Neill hospitality has no limit!

Top: Nothing is out of place in Ellen's inside/outside beachy cottage. Case in point: a little Adirondack-style garden bench from the forties smack dab in the middle of a downstairs sitting room. "Paint it? Never!" answers an astonished Ellen. "It earned that wonderful patina."

Above: An old ruffled and checked pillow ($4) and an unmatched Wedgwood cup ($5) and saucer ($3)—all from Brimfield Market—suggest a comfortable spot for morning tea.

"The bedspreads [pale pink and white chenille] were a precaution-
ary measure to protect the rods inside the piano from dampness,"
insists Robert Miller, its owner. The rest of this surreal still life
consists of gifts from visiting friends. The "fuzzy" blue chair was
"just stuck up there for fun," and then became "incredibly useful
as an easel to prop a photograph or painting against. It invites
ideas," suggests Mr. Miller wryly. "It also stands very well on its
own." Beneath it rests a favorite gift—a fake rock meant for a
home aquarium. The vase to the right, speckled with dots of yellow glaze, is Scandinavian—a gift to themselves that the Millers
bought for less than $10 in "a junk shop" in New York. (You can
read about the pewter lamp on page 185.) Stacked on the balcony
to the left are English metal chairs from the early 1900s, bar-
gained, one by one, out from under the attendants seated on them
in front of various shops in Jamaica. "They were very surprised to
learn of my interest. I paid two dollars or whatever they wanted."
Each retains its original paint, or what's left of it.

Right: Not all of Robert Miller's chairs are in strange places. In fact, the rest are scattered in normal places, such as around a table—"It's an Eames I rescued, about to be thrown out," exclaims Robert Miller—which accommodates many more chairs than the two pulled up to it. "They're both from the fifties—reliable and functional with vinyl seats and shaped iron legs. They have character—they are characters. We found them at a New York City flea market for five dollars each." The painting above the table, entitled Disco, is by Craig Robbins. The lamp is from the fifties. The shiny glazed bowl is a high-school student's work, bought for its "spirited design" by Miller from the Douglas Garden Thrift Shop in Miami Beach for 50 cents.

Below: Another fifties chair, of turquoise vinyl flecked with silver sparkles, stands on tripod legs just outside the kitchen. The Millers picked it up for $10 in a Miami thrift shop no longer in existence.

Left: A fifties bar stool looks like a long-legged Giacometti sculpture in front of a painting by Roberto Juarez, a Miami artist and friend of the Millers (see his gift to the Millers on pages 186–187). The 1950s cot to the left of it, with tubular aluminum legs, resembles the work of the 1930s furniture designer Warren MacArthur.

Below: The Art Deco maple folding chair in the Millers' Miami Beach dining room has an upholstered seat and was found at a local thrift shop for less than $10.

It is a barn like this out back of Parker's Trading Post in Elizabeth City, North Carolina, that can make a treasure seeker like myself dizzy with anticipation! The first instinct is to dive in and check out that stack of old mantelpieces at the left, and the shutter at right, and the little chair balanced on that mountain of stuff above it. A cautionary suggestion: stand outside and look before you leap. Pulling out one old board could start a landslide, with you at the bottom. Ask whoever is responsible to show you what you're interested in. I was tempted to climb (but didn't) through Mr. Parker's shed and another like it. When I asked him for the price of the wreck of a blue chair on the right, he offered it to me as a gift. Knowing when to say "No, thank you" can sometimes be the better part of valor. I looked at it longingly, thanked Mr. Parker, took my other find (see page 167), and never looked back.

JUNK GUIDE

CALIFORNIA

Abell's Auction Company
2613 Yates Avenue
City of Commerce, CA 90040
(213) 724-8102
Wednesday, 9:00 a.m.–4:30 p.m.

Community Thrift Store
625 Valencia Street
San Francisco, CA 94110
(415) 861-4910
Tuesday–Thursday, 10:00 a.m.–7:00 p.m.
Friday–Monday, 10:00 a.m.–6:00 p.m.

Cookin'
339 Divisadero Street
San Francisco, CA 94117
(415) 861-1854
Tuesday–Saturday 12:00–6:30 p.m.
Sunday 1:00–5:00 p.m.

Krims Krams
3611 18th Street
San Francisco, CA
(415) 626-1019
Monday–Friday 1:00–6:30 p.m.
Saturday 12:00–6:30 p.m.
Sunday 12:00–6:00 p.m.

369 Turk Street
San Francisco, CA
(415) 441-5503
Monday–Friday 12:00–6:30 p.m.
Saturday 1:00–6:30 p.m.

**Long Beach Outdoor Antiques
  & Collectibles Market**
Veterans Stadium at Lakewood Boulevard
Long Beach, CA
(213) 655-5703
Third Sunday of every month,
  8:00 a.m.–3:00 p.m.
Admission: $3.50

Ron Meyer Design
7711 Fountain Avenue
Los Angeles, CA 90046
(213) 851-7576

Ohio
1409 Abbot-Kinney Boulevard
Venice, CA 90291
(310) 450-4664
Wednesday–Friday 12:00–6:00 p.m.
Saturday–Sunday 11:00 a.m.–6:00 p.m.

OHIO
in Venice
California 90291

SOLD TO:
Mary
19
NY

ITEM		
striped vases (pair) (35)		
red enamel radio	9 f/set of 4	
hall custard dish		75
old toy tin plates	4 f/set of 2	
childs metal rocker (75)		133

Pasadena City College Flea Market
Hill Avenue between Colorado
   and Del Mar
Pasadena, CA 91106
(818) 585-7906
First Sunday of every month,
   8:00 a.m.–3:00 p.m.
Admission: $5.00

Pink Paraffin
3234 16th Street
San Francisco, CA 94103
(415) 621-7116
Open daily 12:00–6:00 p.m.

Rose Bowl Flea Market
Pasadena, CA
(213) 587-5100
Second Sunday of every month,
   9:00 a.m.–3:00 p.m.
Admission: $5.00

Robert Miles Runyon
Graphic Designer
121 Fifth Street
Manhattan Beach, CA 90266
(310) 379-7232

Sharp Brothers Trading Post
525 Hayes
San Francisco, CA 94102
(415) 864-2756
Monday–Saturday 9:00 a.m.–4:30 p.m.

Such-A-Deal
3915 Telegraph Avenue
Oakland, CA 94609
(415) 655-2508
By appointment only

Union Jack Company
950 Leavenworth
San Francisco, CA 94109
(415) 771-5884

Laurie Warner
Custom made painted furniture
1827 Jewett Drive
Los Angeles, CA 90046
(213) 654-5659

COLORADO

Alderfer's Antiques
101 South Monarch Street
Aspen, CO 81611
(303) 925-5051
November 15–April 15;
 June 5–September 15
Tuesday–Saturday 12:00–6:00 P.M.

FLORIDA

Douglas Garden Thrift Shop
5713 N.W. 27th Avenue
Miami, FL 33142
(305) 635-6753
Monday–Saturday 8:00 a.m.–6:00 p.m.
Sunday 10:00 a.m.–5:00 p.m.

Vanity Novelty Garden
918 Lincoln Road
Miami Beach, FL 33139
(305) 534-6115
Monday–Saturday 1:00–7:00 p.m.

MASSACHUSETTS

Brimfield Market
Route 20
Brimfield, MA 01010
(413) 245-9329
Open three times a year,
 in May, July, and September,
 6:00 a.m.–6:00 p.m. Call for specific
 dates
Admission: $3.00; $7.95 for guide
 (three issues)

Toby's Auction House
823 South New Berlin
New Berlin, MA
(617) 859-9407
Open daily 9:00 a.m.–5:00 p.m.

NEW MEXICO

The Rainbow Man
107 East Palace Avenue
Santa Fe, NM 87501
(505) 982-8706
Monday–Saturday 9:00 a.m.–6:00 p.m.
Sunday 10:00 a.m.–5:00 p.m.

Such A Deal
Junque, funk, furniture

Own Owned and Operated

. sell, trade antiques,
fine furniture

by appt.
Tues. thru Sat.
12–6 pm

3915 Tele
(near BA

EXUMA
POWDER IVORY 199

The Twila Zone
Vintage Clothing - Collectibles
iques - Old Costume Jewelry
nia Dare Trail   JoRuth Patterson
NC 27959   (919) 480-0399

NORTH CAROLINA

Franklin Flea and Craft Market
199 Highlands Road
Franklin, NC 28734
(704) 524-6658
Wednesday, Friday, and Saturday

Jockey Lot Antiques and Flea Markets
Route 6, Box 206C
Elizabeth City, NC 27909
(919) 264-3655
Monday–Thursday 1:00–5:30 p.m.
Friday–Saturday 9:00 a.m.–5:30 p.m.

Parker's Trading Post
1051 U.S. 17 South
Elizabeth City, NC 27909
(919) 335-4896
(919) 338-3700
Monday–Friday 10:00 a.m.–5:00 p.m.
Saturday 12:00–5:00 p.m.

Pontes Antiques
c/o Ocean Blue Services
1903 South Croatan Highway
Kill Devil Hills, NC 27948
(919) 441-5757
Monday–Friday 9:00 a.m.–5:00 p.m.
Saturday 9:00 a.m.–6:00 p.m.

Charles Reber
Woodcarver
West Southside Road
Route 1, Box 81
Nags Head, NC 27959
(919) 441-5307
By appointment only

The Twila Zone
3330 South Virginia Dare Trail
Nags Head, NC 27959
Monday–Saturday 10:30 a.m.–5:00 p.m.
(919) 480-0399

NEW YORK

Bottle Shop Antiques
Route 44
Washington Hollow, NY 12578
(914) 677-3638
Open daily except Tuesday 11:00 a.m.–
  5:00 p.m.

Call Again Thrift Shop
1711 First Avenue
New York, NY 10128
(212) 831-0845
Monday–Saturday 10:00 a.m.–4:30 p.m.

Richard Camp Antiques
Montauk Highway
Wainscott, NY 11975
(516) 537-0330
Call for hours

Anne Keefe Chamberlin Collectibles
County Road 58, Coleman's Station
Millerton, NY 12546
(518) 789-3732/6507
Saturday–Sunday 11:00 a.m.–5:00 p.m.

Collector's Corner
Route 22 and 199, Northeast Center
Millerton, NY 12546
Saturday–Sunday 11:00 a.m.–5:00 p.m.

Copake Country Auction
Box H, Old Route 22
Copake, NY 12516
(518) 329-1142
Monday–Thursday 9:00 a.m.–4:00 p.m.

Fishs Eddy
551 Hudson Street
New York, NY 10014
(212) 627-3956
889 Broadway
New York, NY 10003
(212) 420-9020
Open daily 12:00–7:00 p.m.

Flying Duck Outdoor Sporting Collectibles
R.D. Box 109
Stuyvesant, NY 12173
(518) 758-7257
Saturday–Sunday 10:00 a.m.–5:00 p.m.

Howard Frisch
New and Antiquarian Books
Old Post Road
Livingston, NY 12541
(518) 851-7493
Friday–Sunday 11:00 a.m.–4:00 p.m.

Richard Giglio
Artist specializing in
    black-and-white paintings
2231 Broadway
New York, NY 10024
(212) 724-8118

Housing Works Thrift Shop
136 West 18 Street
New York, NY 10011
(212) 366-0820
Monday—Saturday 10:00 a.m.—6:00 p.m.

Johnson & Johnson Antiques
Box 361, Route 22 North
Millerton, NY 12546
(518) 789-3848
Friday—Sunday 10:00 a.m.—5:00 p.m.

Kelter Malcé
74 Jane Street
New York, NY 10014
(212) 675-7380
By appointment only

Kitschen
15 Christopher Street
New York, NY 10014
(212) 727-0430
Tuesday—Sunday 1:00—8:00 p.m.

LA-Z-BOY Antiques
236 West 10 Street
New York, NY 10014
(212) 627-5442
Call for hours

Millbrook Antiques Mall
Franklin Avenue
P.O. Box 1267
Millbrook, NY 12545
(914) 677-9311
Monday—Saturday 11:00 a.m.—5:00 p.m.
Sunday 1:00—5:00 p.m.

PJ Flea Market
348½ Warren Street
Hudson, NY 12534
(518) 828-2271
Open daily 9:00 a.m.—5:00 p.m.

Praiseworthy Antiques
Main Street
Guilford, NY 12780
(607) 895-6211
Thursday—Monday 10:00 a.m.—5:00 p.m.

Alice & Don Reid's
     Antiques in the Barn
P.O. Box 113
Livingston, NY 12541
(518) 851-9177
Call for hours

Alice & Don Reid's at the
     Hudson Antiques Center
536 Warren Street
Hudson, NY 12534
(518) 828-9920

John Ralbovsky
Scenic Artist
307 72 Street, #1D
Brooklyn, NY 11209
(718) 836-2577

Rodgers Book Barn
Rodman Road
Craryville, NY 12521
(518) 325-3610
Saturday—Sunday 10:00 a.m.—6:00 p.m.
Monday—Friday (July and August only)
     12:00—6:00 p.m.

Paula Rubenstein, Ltd.
65 Prince Street
New York, NY 10012
(212) 966-8954
Monday—Saturday 12:30—6:30 p.m.

Ruby Beets
Poxybogue Road and Route 27
Bridgehampton, NY 11932
(516) 537-2802
Thursday—Sunday 11:00 a.m.—5:00 p.m.

Sage Street Antiques
Route 114 (Sage and Division Streets)
Sag Harbor, NY 11963
(516) 725-4036
Saturday 11:00 a.m.—5:00 p.m.
Sunday 1:00 p.m.—5:00 p.m.

Stepping Stones
Route 9G
Germantown, NY 12526
(518) 851-7536
Monday—Friday 10:00 a.m.—4:00 p.m.

22 Junk-A-Tique
Route 22
Millerton, NY 12546
(518) 675-7380
Thursday—Sunday 1:00—5:00 p.m.

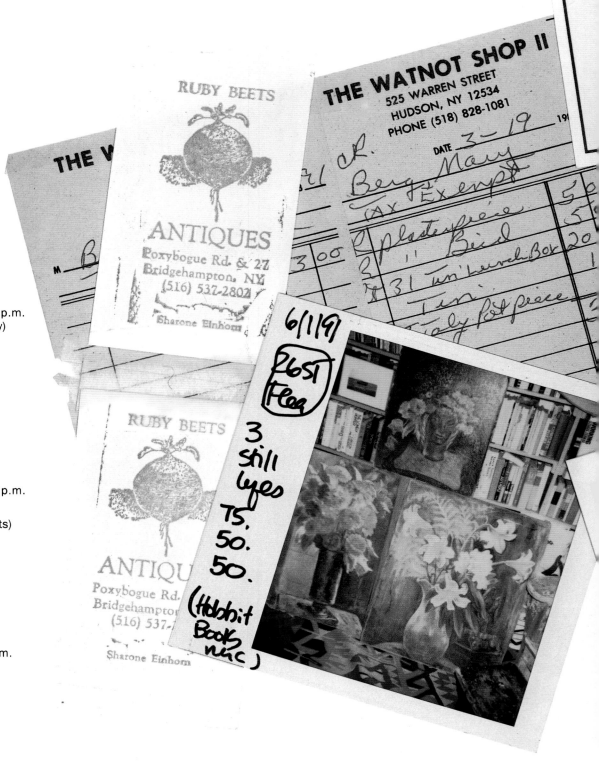

U.S.E.D.
17 PERRY ST.
N.Y., N.Y. 10014

Rodgers **BOOK BARN**
(518) 325-3610
Hillsdale, N.Y. 12529

One Mile
WEST END RD
ROOMAN RD
WHIPPOORWILL RD
Route 22
NEW YORK MASSACHUSETTS
Taconic Pkwy.
Church
Route 23
CRARYVILLE
HILLSDALE
Gt. Barrington

**Old & Unusual Books
Paperbacks & Records
Bought & Sold**

OPEN ALL YEAR: Sat. & Sun. 10 am - 6 pm
July - August, Mon. - Fri. 12 - 6

Doll shop -12   26 rist
Daun Grannettie $15 with boleo

Stepping Stones
COLLECTIBLES
ANTIQUES
(518) 851-7536

Twenty-sixth Street Flea Market
Twenty-sixth Street and Sixth Avenue
New York, NY
Saturday—Sunday 9:00 a.m.—9:00 p.m.
Admission: $1.00

U.S.E.D.
17 Perry Street
New York, NY 10014
(212) 627-0730
Open daily 12:30—8:00 p.m.

Judyth VanAmringe
448 West 37 Street
New York, NY 10018
(212) 736-5130
By appointment only

The Watnot Shop II
525 Warren Street
Hudson, NY 12534
(518) 828-1081

TEXAS

Room Service
6200 Richmond Avenue
Houston, TX
(713) 952-8200
Monday—Friday 10:00 a.m.—2:00 p.m.;
    5:00—10:00 p.m.
Saturday—Sunday 4:00—10:00 p.m.

VIRGINIA

Cecil's Antiques
7 West Broad Street
Richmond, VA 23220
(804) 643-9273
Monday—Saturday 9:30 a.m.—5:30 p.m.

Stuckey's Antique Emporium
315 West Broad Street
Richmond, VA 23220
(804) 643-4892
Monday—Saturday 10:00 a.m.—5:00 p.m.

NEWSPAPERS, DIRECTORIES, AND GUIDES TO FLEA MARKETS, AUCTIONS, SWAPS, AND SHOPS

Antiques & The Arts Weekly
Bee Publishing Company
5 Church Hill Road
Newtown, CT 06470
(203) 426-3141
Weekly newspaper listing major antique shows, auctions, and markets across the country; $38.00 per year

Clark's Flea Market U.S.A.
2156 Cotton Patch Lane
Milton, FL 32570
(904) 623-0794
A national directory of flea markets and swap meets; $7.50 per issue or $25.00 per year (four issues)

The Great American Flea Market Directory
Cranbook House
P.O. Box 6002
Saginaw, MI 48608
A directory for the professional flea-market vendor who travels the country to sell his wares; $10.45

Maine Antiques Digest
P.O. Box 1429
Waldoboro, ME 04572
(207) 832-4888
A monthly newspaper that lists flea markets in the U.S. and abroad; $29.00 for 12 issues

Never Buy Anything New
Heyday Books
P.O. Box 9145
Berkeley, CA 94709
(510) 549-3564
A guide to 400 second-hand, thrift, and consignment stores in the San Francisco Bay area; $9.95

The Official Directory to U.S. Flea Markets
House of Collectibles
201 East 50 Street
New York, NY 10022
(212) 751-2600
A directory that provides essential information about flea markets nationwide; $5.99

"SPECIAL" JUNK NIGHT

rday, January 11, 6 PM SHARP!

HELD AT OUR GALLERY
16 Livingston Street • Saugerties, N.Y.
Centrally located between NYC and Albany
ew York State Thruway to Exit 20; take ___ mile to center of ___
___en right onto Livin___ ___ ___torag___

THE
SAN FRANCISCO
Thrift and Wisdom
ALMANAC

San Francisco's Native Wisdo___

Now Just $6.95!

Editor, Walter Biller

ISBN 0-9628427-1-0

ISSN# 1053-1696

ATTENTION! TAG SALERS! HAVE YOUR TAG SALE WITH US AT THE NORH'S
ARK ANTIQUE CENTER ON ROUTE 9 IN FISHKILL ON SATURDAY & SUNDAY JULY
18 & 19. Be exposed to Hundreds and Hundreds of Buyers. We do the
Advertising. You just Set-up and Sell. A Spot for (1) Day, $25; (2) Days, $45. Call
Rick Lawler at 914-897-4830 for details.
___bottle current retail, (10) 9oz. bottles
3M IMAGING POWDER #412: $76 per bottle ___ for $49 per bottle. COPY PAPER
___ilable, will sacrifice for $59 per bottle ___ $57 ___

An ode to "junk" by a young forager-poet -- Liz's nephew. She dropped it off thinking I might enjoy it — YES!!! (save for book!)

```
                    JUNK

      Some people say it's garbage

      Some people say it's junk

      A little boat with a hole I caught before it sunk

      A wad of bubble gum covered with green mold

      An ice cream cone that wouldn't quite stay cold

      A rusty bolt from a tattered old trunk

      I think it's treasure. ...but they call it junk!


                            Adam Bushnoe
                            9 years old
                            Clay, New York
                            10/21/88
```